MW01489018

2023 Official Baseball Rules Study Guide

By Troy Ray Grimes
Marathon Ump

Britannica defines baseball as a game played with a bat, a ball, and gloves between two teams of nine players each on a field with four white bases laid out in a diamond (i.e., a square oriented so that its diagonal line is vertical). Teams alternate positions as batters (offense) and fielders (defense), exchanging places when three members of the batting team are "put out." As batters, players try to hit the ball out of the reach of the fielding team and make a complete circuit around the bases for a "run." The team that scores the most runs in nine innings (times at bat) wins the game.

Pretty simple game. Or is it?

The many, many rules that it takes to simply "play ball" is enormous. *Marathon Ump's 2023 Official Baseball Rules Study Guide* breaks down these complex rules and will help you become a "baseball rule expert".

Whether you are an umpire and want to use this study guide like batting practice to stay sharp, a player or coach that wants to better themselves by better understanding the Great Game, or simply a baseball nerd that wants to know as much about the game as possible - this book will have lots for you.

The study guide covers each and every rule section of the Official Baseball Rules. First test your knowledge by answering challenging multiple choice questions. Then grade yourself with the answers that are shown at the back of the book along with their detailed explanations. You will also be provided a link to "play online", where 25 questions will be randomly drawn from all sections of the Official Rules. The on-line exam will "grade" you for each section of the rule book and can be taken an unlimited number of times.

In this study guide, you will learn:

- The surprisingly complex rules on using a designated hitter in the line up.
- When is the batter allowed and not allowed to advance to first base on a dropped third strike. (Probably the most misunderstood rule in Youth Leagues).
- What happens when a ball in play hits the umpire (besides the umpire getting a loud round of boos).
- When does the run count on a play that the third out of the inning is made.
- What is the definition of "first play by an infielder" and in what situation is it extremely important?
- What is the difference between the "Infield Fly Rule" and a "intentionally dropped ball" and what situations do each come into play.
- What happens when a player bats out of order, including understanding the terms "proper batter" and "improper batter".
- What is and isn't a balk.
- What happens when Catcher Interference is called?
- If the batter interferes with the catcher attempting to throw out a runner stealing, who is out?
- And much, much more.

Marathon Ump's 2023 Official Baseball Rules Study Guide covers rule changes for the 2023 MLB season including:

- New measurements for first, second, and third base
- When is a position player allowed to pitch?
- New defensive restrictions (i.e. "outlawing the shift")
- Parameters for extra inning games (i.e. "ghost runners)
- New "Time Clock" rules including violations for both pitchers and batters.
- New restrictions for the pitcher on attempted pick offs.

Table of Contents

*   Includes new measurements for first, second, and third base

**   Includes when a position player is allowed to pitch

***   Includes "outlawing the shift"

**** Includes "ghost runners" in extra innings

2.00 The Playing Field

1: The infield is a ____ foot square

    A. 80
    B. 85
    C. 90
    D. 95

2: Any playing field constructed by a professional club after June 1, 1958 shall provide a minimum distance of _____ feet from home base to the nearest fence, stand or other obstruction on the right and left field foul lines.

    A. 300
    B. 310
    C. 325
    D. 350

3: Any playing field constructed by a professional club after June 1, 1958 shall provide a minimum distance of _____ feet to the center field fence.

      A. 380
      B. 390
      C. 400
      D. 410

4: Home base is a _____ inch square.

      A. 17
      B. 18
      C. 19
      D. 20

5: Beginning in 2023, the bases are a _____ inch square.

      A. 15
      B. 16
      C. 17
      D. 18

6: The pitcher's plate is _____ inches by 6 inches.

      A. 21
      B. 22
      C. 23
      D. 24

3.00 Equipment and Uniform

1: If a player intentionally discolors or damages the ball by rubbing it with soil, rosin, sand-paper, etc the player will be rejected from the game and automatically suspended for _____ games.

       A. 1
       B. 3
       C. 10
       D. 15

2: The bat may not be covered for more than _____ inches from its end with any substance to improve the grip (i.e. pine tar).

       A. 16
       B. 18
       C. 20

3: If a player is discovered to be using a bat with pine tar above the legal limit, the batter is automatically out and ejected from the game.

       A. True
       B. False

4: A catcher may not use a mitt that is more than _____ inches in circumference.

    A. 32
    B. 34
    C. 36
    D. 38

5: A first baseman may not use a glove that is more than _____ inches long from top to bottom.

    A. 12
    B. 13
    C. 14

6: All players in both the Major Leagues and Minor Leagues must wear a double ear flap helmet while at bat.

    A. True
    B. False

7: All base coaches in both the Major Leagues and Minor Leagues must wear a protective helmet.

    A. True
    B. False

4.00 Game Preliminaries

4.03 Exchange of Lineup Cards

1: From Opening day through August 31 of the championship season and during postseason games, Major League Clubs may designate a maximum of _____ pitchers for a game.

     A. 12
     B. 13
     C. 14
     D. 15

2: From September 1 through the end of the championship season (including any tiebreaker games), Major League Clubs may designate a maximum of _____ pitchers for a game.

     A. 12
     B. 13
     C. 14
     D. 15

3: Players who qualify as "Two-Way Players" under Major League Rule 2(b)(2) may appear as pitchers during a game without counting toward a club's pitcher limitations.

     A. True
     B. False

4: A position player (a player not designated as a pitcher or two-way player on the lineup card) may come into pitch for his team if his team is losing by ___ runs or more or in extra innings.

   A. 7
   B. 8
   C. 9
   D. 10

5: A position player (a player not designated as a pitcher or two-way player on the lineup card) may come into pitch for his team if his team is winning by ___ runs or more in the 9th inning.

   A. 7
   B. 8
   C. 9
   D. 10

6: The _____ shall make certain that the original and copies of the respective batting orders are identical.

      A. Home team general manager
      B. Home team field manager
      C. Umpire-in-chief

7: Unless the home club has given previous notice that the game has been postponed or will be delayed in starting, the umpires shall enter the playing field _____ minute(s) before the hour set for the game to begin and proceed directly to home base where they shall be met by the managers of the opposing teams.

      A. 1
      B. 5
      C. 10
      D. 15

8: At the pre-game home plate meeting between umpires and managers, the _____ manager (or his designee) shall give his batting order to the umpire-in-chief first.

    A. Visiting team
    B. Home team

9: Lineup cards presented to the umpire-in-chief by a manager in the pre-game meeting must list the fielding positions to be played by each player in the batting order.

    A. True
    B. False

10: Lineup cards presented to the umpire-in-chief by a manager in the pre-game meeting should not list a designated hitter that is in the starting lineup since there is no applicable fielding position for them.

    A. True
    B. False

11: Failure to list a potential substitute player in the lineup card presented to the umpire-in-chief by a manager in the pre-game meeting shall make such potential substitute player ineligible to enter the game.

    A. True
    B. False

12: At what point of the game does the umpire-in-chief gain sole authority to determine when the game shall be called, suspended or resumed on account of weather or the condition of the playing field.

    A. 30 minutes before game time.
    B. First pitch of the game.
    C. When the home team's batting order is handed to umpire-in-chief

13: The umpire-in-chief shall not call the game until at least _____ minutes after he has suspended play.

     A. 15
     B. 30
     C. 45
     D. 60

4.04 Weather and Field Conditions

1: Before the exchange of lineup cards, the _____ shall be the sole judge as to whether a game shall not be started because of unsuitable weather conditions or the unfit conditions of the playing field, except for the second game of a conventional or split doubleheader.

     A. Umpire-in-Chief
     B. Home team
     C. MLB corporate office

2: The _____ shall be the sole judge as to whether the second game of a conventional or split doubleheader shall not be started because of unsuitable weather conditions or the unfit conditions of the playing field.

     A. Umpire-in-Chief of first game
     B. Home team
     C. MLB corporate office

4.08 Doubleheaders

1: The second game of a doubleheader shall start _____ minutes after the first game is completed, unless a longer interval (not to exceed _____ minutes) is declared by the umpire-in-chief and announced to the opposing managers at end of the first game.

      A. 15, 30
      B. 30, 45
      C. 30, 60
      D. 45, 60

2: When a rescheduled game is part of a doubleheader, the rescheduled game shall be the first game, and the second game shall be the regularly scheduled game for that date.

      A. True
      B. False

5.00 - Playing the Game

5.02: Fielding Positions

1: When a pitcher begins his delivery of the ball to the batter, the defensive team must have a minimum of ____ players (in addition to pitcher and catcher) with both feet completely in front of the outer boundary of the infield dirt.

    A. 2
    B. 3
    C. 4

2: The pitcher begins his motion to the plate when there are 3 infielders on the left side of the infield and an "illegal shift" is called. The batter does not swing at the pitch.

    A. Pitch is automatically called a "ball".
    B. Pitch is called a "no pitch".
    C. Batter is awarded first base.

<u>3:</u>

```
Balls      1
Strikes    2
Outs       1
```

Runner on 3rd

The pitcher begins his motion to the plate when there are 3 infielders on the left side of the infield and an "illegal shift" is called. The batter swings at the pitch anyway and hits a fly ball to the outfield that is caught by the right fielder. R3 tags up and crosses home plate.

       A. The ball is dead as soon as the "illegal shift" is called. The batter is awarded 1st base and R3 must return to 3rd base, no run can score on this play.
       B. The batter is awarded 1st base on the play, and the run counts.
       C. Manager of the offense may elect to decline the "illegal shift" call and accept the play resulting in the batter being out and the run counting.

5.05: When the Batter Becomes a Runner

<u>1:</u> A pitch bounces in front of home plate, then is hit fair by the batter.

       A. Pitch is considered a ball, and the batter returns to bat (or awarded first if ball four).
       B. It is a fair ball and the batter becomes a runner.
       C. Is considered a foul ball.

<u>2:</u>

```
Balls      2
Strikes    2
Outs       1
```

Runners on 1st and 2nd

Next pitch is a swinging strike on the batter that is not caught by the catcher. Batter may attempt to advance to 1st base.

       A. True
       B. False

<u>3:</u>

Balls   2
Strikes   2
Outs   2

Runners on 1st and 2nd

Next pitch is a called strike and is not caught by the catcher. Batter may attempt to advance to 1st base.

  A. True
  B. False

<u>4:</u>

Balls   2
Strikes   2
Outs   0

Runners on 2nd and 3rd

Next pitch is a swinging strike that is not caught by the catcher. Batter may attempt to advance to 1st base.

  A. True
  B. False

<u>5:</u>

Balls   2
Strikes   2
Outs   0

No Runners on base

Next pitch is a called strike on the batter that is not caught by the catcher. Batter may attempt to advance to 1st base.

  A. True
  B. False

<u>6 :</u> The only time a batter may attempt to advance to 1st base when a third strike is not caught by the catcher is when there are two outs.

    A. True
    B. False

<u>7 :</u> If a pitch touches the ground, then hits the batter -

    A. It is a ball.
    B. Batter is awarded first base.

<u>8 :</u> Batter hits a fair ball through the infield past the 2nd baseman and the ball subsequently hits the umpire stationed in shallow outfield -

    A. Batter is out.
    B. Batter becomes a runner, and may advance as many bases as possible.
    C. Ball is dead, and the batter is awarded first base.

<u>9 :</u> If a fair fly ball is deflected by a fielder into the stands, or over the fence into *foul* territory -

        A. Batter is entitled to advance to second base.
        B. Batter is entitled to a home run.

<u>10 :</u> If a fair fly ball is deflected by a fielder into the stands, or over the fence into *fair* territory

        A. Batter is entitled to advance to second base.
        B. Batter is entitled to a home run.

5.06 Running the Bases

5.06(b) Advancing Bases

<u>1:</u>

Balls	2
Strikes	2
Outs	0

Runners on 1st and 2nd

On the next pitch, the batter hits a clean single to center field. R2, thinking the ball is going to be caught, never leaves 2nd base. R1 reaches 2nd base before the ball is returned to the infield. At this point both R1 and R2 are standing on 2nd base. Shortstop tags both R1 and R2. Who is out?

      A. R1
      B. R2
      C. Both R1 and R2.

<u>2:</u>

Balls	2
Strikes	2
Outs	0

Runner on 2nd

Batter hits a deep fly ball to center field that falls in for a hit. R2, thinking the ball is going to be caught, never leaves 2nd base. Batter-runner reaches 2nd base before the ball is returned to the infield. At this point both R2 and the batter-runner are standing on 2nd base. Shortstop tags both R1 and R2. Who is out?

      A. R2.
      B. Batter-runner.
      C. Both R2 and batter-runner

3:

```
Balls      3
Strikes    2
Outs       2
```

Bases loaded

On the next pitch, the batter takes Ball 4. R2 is overzealous and runs past third base toward home and is tagged out on a throw by the catcher before R3 reaches home plate (R3 does touch home).

      A. The run counts
      B. The run does not count

4 : First baseman catches a fly pop near the dugout then falls into the dugout (dugout is considered out of play).

      A. All runners advance one base.
      B. All runners advance two bases.
      C. Runners may only advance if it is a force situation.
      D. Runners do not advance.

5:

```
Balls      3
Strikes    2
Outs       0
```

Runner on 1st

On the next pitch, R1 is attempting to steal. Batter takes ball four, and the pitch gets by the catcher. R1 heads to 3rd, but misses 2nd base. R1 realizes he missed 2nd, and tries to get back to 2nd. Catcher throws ball to 2nd baseman who touches 2nd base before R1 gets back to 2nd (but does not tag R1).

      A. R1 is out.
      B. R1 is not out since he is entitled to 2nd base by being forced there by ball 4.
      C. R1 is no longer entitled to 2nd base because he attempted to go to third, but he is not out because the 2nd baseman did not tag him (not a force play at 2nd).

<u>**6:**</u>

```
Balls      3
Strikes    2
Outs       0
```

Bases loaded

On the next pitch, the batter hits a fly ball in fair territory and the right fielder deliberately throws his glove at the ball and hits the ball while in flight.

      A. Ball is dead, all runners advance 2 bases including the batter runner - i.e., 2 runs score, runners now on 2nd and 3rd.
      B. Ball is dead, all runners advance 3 bases including the batter runner - i.e., 3 runs score, runner now on 3rd.
      C. Ball is live, all runners advance 3 bases (i.e, 3 runs score), batter-runner may advance to home base at his peril.

<u>**7:**</u>

```
Balls      3
Strikes    2
Outs       0
```

Runner on 1st

On the next pitch, R1 is stealing. Batter hits a slow roller down 3rd base line. R1 is past 2nd base and heading to 3rd when the 3rd baseman fields the ball and immediately throws to 1st base (makes the throw before the batter-runner reaches 1st base). The throw is wild and bounces out of play into the stands.

      A. R1 is awarded 3rd base.
      B. R1 is allowed to score.

8:

```
Balls      3
Strikes    2
Outs       0
```

Runner on 1st

R1 is stealing. Batter hits a slow roller down third base line. R1 is past 2nd base and heading to 3rd when the 3rd baseman fields the ball. The 3rd baseman takes a couple of steps toward R1 in an attempt to tag him. R1 stops, so the 3rd baseman throws to 1st base instead. The throw is wild and bounces out of play into the stands.

    A. R1 is awarded 3rd base.
    B. R1 is allowed to score.

9:

```
Balls      3
Strikes    2
Outs       0
```

Runner on 1st

R1 is stealing. Batter slaps a base hit to center field. R1 is past 2nd base and heading to 3rd when the centerfielder fields the ball. The centerfielder immediately throws to 3rd base in an attempt to throw out R1. The throw is wild and bounces out of play into the stands.

    A. R1 is awarded 3rd base.
    B. R1 is allowed to score.

10:

```
Balls      3
Strikes    2
Outs       0
```

Runner on 1st

While engaged with the pitcher's plate, the pitcher makes a legal pick off attempt at first base. The pick off attempt is wild and the ball bounces out of play into the stands.

  A. R1 is awarded 2nd base.
  B. R1 is awarded 3rd base.

11:

```
Balls      3
Strikes    2
Outs       0
```

Runner on 3rd

On the next pitch, the batter hits a fly ball to the right fielder. Thinking the ball is not going to be caught, R3 breaks for home. Right fielder catches the ball and immediately throws to 3rd in an attempt to catch R3. The throw is wild and bounces out of play into the stands. R3 is awarded home on the wild throw. He touches home without ever returning to retouch 3rd base. Defense makes an appeal by throwing to 3rd, saying R3 did not tag up after the catch.

  A. Run scores. R3 did not have to tag up since he was awarded home on the overthrow.
  B. R3 is out.

12:

```
Balls      3
Strikes    2
Outs       0
```

Runner on 1st

Pitcher makes a legal pickoff attempt while engaged with the pitcher's plate, but throws wild and the ball goes out of play.

      A. R1 remains on 1st.
      B. R1 is awarded 2nd base.
      C. R1 is awarded 3rd base.

13:

```
Balls      3
Strikes    2
Outs       0
```

Runner on 1st

Runner on 1st, no outs. Pitcher legally disengages the pitcher's plate and attempts to pick off the runner at 1st. The throw is wild and the ball goes out of play.

      A. R1 remains on 1st.
      B. R1 is awarded 2nd base.
      C. R1 is awarded 3rd base.

14: Batter is hit with a pitch outside the strike zone. The ball is dead, batter is awarded 1st base, and the base runners:

      A. advance one base in all cases.
      B. advance one base only if forced to advance.

15: If a fielder deliberately throws his glove and touches a *thrown ball*, it is:

      A. One base award.
      B. Two base award.
      C. Three base award.

16:

```
Balls     2
Strikes   1
Outs      1
```

Runner on 2nd

On the next pitch, the batter hits an infield pop that hits R2 while R2 is still standing on 2nd base (hits R2 before it has passed an infielder).

    A. Batter is out, R2 remains at 2nd base.
    B. R2 is out, batter is returned to bat with one strike added to the count.
    C. R2 is out, the batter is awarded 1st base.
    D. Both R2 and the batter are out.

17:

```
Balls     2
Strikes   1
Outs      1
```

Runners on 1st and 2nd

On the next pitch, the batter hits a routine infield pop (infield fly is called) that hits R2 while *R2 is still standing on 2nd base.*

    A. Batter is out (on infield fly rule), R2 remains at 2nd base.
    B. R2 is out, batter is returned to bat with one strike added to the count.
    C. R2 is out, the batter is awarded 1st base.
    D. Both R2 and the batter are out.

```
Balls      2
Strikes    1
Outs       1
```

Runners on 1st and 2nd

On the next pitch, the batter hits a routine infield pop (infield fly is called) that hits R2 while R2 *is off of 2nd base.*

    A. Batter is out (on infield fly rule), R2 remains at 2nd base.
    B. R2 is out, batter is returned to bat with one strike added to the count.
    C. R2 is out, the batter is awarded 1st base.
    D. Both R2 and the batter are out.

19:

```
Balls      2
Strikes    1
Outs       1
```

Runners on 1st and 2nd

On the next pitch, the batter hits a line drive toward the pitcher. Pitcher deflects the ball, the ball hits off of R2 a couple of steps off of 2nd base, and then is caught by the shortstop before the ball ever touches the ground.

    A. This is a legal catch, R2 can be doubled off of 2nd if he does not get back in time.
    B. No catch. Once the ball bounces off the runner it is treated as if it had touched the ground.

5.06(c) Dead Balls

1: If a fair ball touches an umpire before it has passed an infielder other than the pitcher, it is considered a dead ball and runners advance if forced.

    A. True
    B. False

2: If a fair ball touches an umpire after it has passed an infielder other than the pitcher, it is considered a dead ball and runners advance if forced.

    A. True
    B. False

3:

```
Balls       2
Strikes     2
Outs        0

Bases empty.
```

On the next pitch, the batter swings and misses for strike three. Pitch gets by the catcher, but rebounds off the umpire. Catcher catches the rebound before it hits the ground. Batter may attempt to advance to first base.

    A. True
    B. False

4:

```
Balls      2
Strikes    1
Outs       0

Runner on 1st
```

The next pitch gets past the catcher, and lodges in the umpire's mask.   Runner is awarded 2nd base.

A. True
B. False

5.07 Pitching

5.07(a) Legal Pitching Delivery

1: There are two legal pitching positions, the windup position and the _____ position.

2: Pitchers can not take signs from the catcher while in contact with the pitcher's plate.

     A. True
     B. False

3: When a pitcher holds the ball with both hands in front of his body with his pivot foot in contact with the pitcher's plate and his other foot free, he is considered to be:

     A. In the windup position.
     B. In the set position.

4: In the windup position, a pitcher is not permitted to have both feet in contact with the pitcher's plate.

     A. True
     B. False

5: From the windup position, a pitcher may step and throw to a base in an attempt to pick-off a runner without committing a balk.

     A. True
     B. False

6: From the set position, a pitcher may legally disengage from the pitcher's plate by stepping backward or forward with his pivot foot.

      A. True
      B. False

7: From the set position, the pitcher is required to come to a complete stop after his stretch even if there are no runners on base.

      A. True
      B. False

5.07(d) Throwing to the Bases

1: Runner on 1st. Pitcher, from set position, attempts to pick off runner with a snap throw followed by a step directly toward 1st base.   This is legal, and not a balk.

      A. True
      B. False

2: If a pitcher, from the set position, removes his pivot foot from contact with the pitcher's plate by stepping backward with that foot, he is now considered to be an infielder.

      A. True
      B. False

3: An ambidextrous pitcher is allowed to switch pitching arms whenever he wants during a single at-bat to the same batter.

    A. True
    B. False

5.08 How a Team Scores

1:

Balls	2
Strikes	1
Outs	2

Bases Loaded

Batter hits a ground ball to deep third. Third baseman fields the ball and beats R2 to third for the force out. R3, with a huge jump, crosses home plate before the force play is made at third. The run counts.

    A. True
    B. False

2:

Balls	2
Strikes	1
Outs	2

Runners on 2nd and 3rd

Batter hits a ground ball to deep third. Third baseman fields the ball and tags R2 coming into third base. R3, with a huge jump, crosses home plate before the tag is applied on R2 at third. The run counts.

    A. True
    B. False

<u>**3:**</u>

```
Balls      2
Strikes    1
Outs       2
```

Runner on 3rd

Batter hits a ground ball to deep short. Shortstop fields the ball and throws the batter out at first by half-step. R3, with a huge jump, crosses home plate before the play is made at first. The run counts.

      A. True
      B. False

<u>**4:**</u>

```
Balls      2
Strikes    1
Outs       1
```

Runners on 1st and 2nd

On the next pitch, the batter hits an inside the park home run. R2 misses third, and is called out on appeal. Two runs count.

      A. True
      B. False

```
Balls       2
Strikes     1
Outs        2
```

Runners on 1st and 2nd

On the next pitch, the batter hits an inside the park home run. R2 misses third, and is called out on appeal. Two runs count.

      A. True
      B. False

6:

```
Balls       2
Strikes     1
Outs        2
```

Bases loaded

On the next pitch, the batter hits a grand slam home run. On appeal, the batter is declared out for missing first base.   How many runs count.

      A. 0
      B. 1
      C. 2
      D. 3

5.09 Making an Out

5.09(a) Retiring the Batter

1: First baseman, on a foul pop near the dugout, reaches into the dugout (without stepping into it) to make the catch. The batter is out.

    A. True
    B. False

2: First baseman, on a foul pop near the dugout, has one foot on the ground in play and one foot over the inside of the dugout (but not touching the ground inside the dugout) when he makes the catch. Legal catch, batter is out.

    A. True
    B. False

3: Center fielder is racing back on a deep fly ball. He makes the catch and immediately runs into the fence which causes him to drop the ball. The batter is out.

    A. True
    B. False

4: To make a legal catch, the fielder must hold the ball long enough to prove that he has complete control of the ball and that his release of the ball is voluntary and

_____.

5: Center fielder and right fielder converge on a fly ball. Center fielder is first to touch the ball. He juggles the ball and drops it. Right fielder catches it before it hits the ground.

    A. No catch - ball is live.
    B. Legal catch- runners may leave their bases at the point when the right fielder makes the catch.
    C. Legal catch- runners may leave their bases at the point center fielder first touched the ball.

6: Right fielder is chasing down a foul ball near the stands. He hops on top of the tarp that is stored in play along the grandstand fence. He makes the catch while standing on top of the tarp with both feet. The batter is out.

      A. True
      B. False

7: Right fielder is chasing down a foul ball near the stands. He reaches into the stands in an attempt to make the catch. A fan prevents him from making the catch. The batter is out on fan interference.

      A. True
      B. False

8: Right fielder is chasing down a foul ball near the stands. A fan reaches out over the playing field and prevents the right fielder from making the catch. The batter is out on fan interference.

      A. True
      B. False

9: No one on base. Two outs. Batter takes strike three. Catcher misses the catch, the ball hits his chest protector, and he traps it against his chest before the ball hits the ground.

      A. Batter may attempt to advance to 1st base.
      B. Strike three - batter is out.

10: Batter hits a pitch. The ball bounces and hits him while he is still in the batter's box.

      A. Foul ball.
      B. Batter is out.

11: Batter hits a pitch. The ball bounces and hits him after he has left the batter's box.

      A. Foul ball.
      B. Batter is out.

12: Batter hits a dribbler in fair territory. Batter drops his bat and the ball rolls against the bat in fair territory. There was no intention by the batter to interfere with the course of the ball. What is the call?

    A. Ball is live. Batter-runner may continue to advance around the bases.
    B. Ball is dead. Batter-runner is awarded first base.
    C. Batter is out.
    D. Ruled a foul ball.

13: Batter hits an infield pop-up and accidentally without any intent throws his bat on the swing. The thrown bat interferes with the infielder attempting to make the catch. What is the call?

    A. Batter is out.
    B. Ball is live. Batter-runner may continue to advance around the bases.
    C. Is ruled a "no play" - batter returns to bat.

14:

```
Balls     2
Strikes   1
Outs      1
```

Runners on 1st and 3rd

On the next pitch, the batter hits a pop up to 2nd baseman. The 2nd baseman intentionally drops the pop up (after making contact with the ball). What is the call?

    A. Ball is dead - batter is out, runners are returned to 1st and 3rd.
    B. Legal play by 2nd baseman because infield fly rule is not applicable in this situation.
    C. Ball is dead - batter is awarded first base. R1 is awarded 2nd base since he is forced. R3 remains on third (bases now loaded).

15:

```
Balls      2
Strikes    1
Outs       1
```

Runners on 1st and 3rd

On the next pitch, the batter hits a pop up to 2nd baseman. The 2nd baseman intentionally lets the pop-up drop without touching the ball before it hits the ground. What is the call?

   A. Ball is dead - batter is out, runners are returned to 1st and 3rd.
   B. Legal play - ball is live and in play.
   C. Ball is dead - batter is awarded first base. R1 is awarded 2nd base since he is forced. R3 remains on third (bases now loaded).

16:

```
Balls      1
Strikes    2
Outs       2
```

Runner on 3rd

On the next pitch, R3 attempts to steal home. The pitch hits R3 in the strike zone. What is the call?

   A. Strike 3 on batter, 3 outs, run does not count
   B. Strike 3 on batter, 3 outs, run counts.
   C. Ruled a no pitch, run counts, batter remains at bat with 1 ball 2 strike count.
   D. Pitch is called a ball, run counts, batter remains at bat with 2 ball 2 strike count.

17:

```
Balls      1
Strikes    2
Outs       1
```

Runner on 3rd

On next pitch, R3 attempts to steal home. The pitch hits R3 in the strike zone. What is the call?

    A. Strike 3 on batter, 2 outs, run does not count.
    B. Strike 3 on batter, 2 outs, run counts.
    C. Ruled a no pitch, run counts, batter remains at bat with 1 ball 2 strike count.
    D. Pitch is called a ball, run counts, batter remains at bat with 2 ball 2 strike count.

5.09(b) Retiring a Runner

1: Bottom of ninth, scored tied. Runner on 1st, one out. Batter hits an apparent game winning home run. R1, thinking this automatically wins the game, cuts across the field toward his bench as the batter-runner circles the bases. What is the call?

    A. R1 is out for abandoning his effort to run the bases, batter-runner is out for passing R1. No runs count. Play continues to the top of the 10th inning.
    B. R1 is out for abandoning his effort to run the bases, batter-runner is not out but his run does not count. Play continues to the bottom of the 9th inning with 2 outs and scored tied.
    C. R1 is out for abandoning his effort to run the bases. Batter-runner run counts. Game over, the home team wins by one run.
    D. Both runs count. Base runners do not have to have run the bases on a game winning home run.

2: If a runner falsely believes he is out on a close play at first base and starts for the dugout and progresses a reasonable distance, he will be declared out for abandoning the bases even if no tag is applied.

    A. True
    B. False

3:

```
Balls     1
Strikes   1
Outs      1
```

Runner on 1st

On the next pitch, R1 is stealing. Batter hits a foul tip that is caught by the catcher. Catcher makes no attempt to throw out the runner. R1 must return to first because the foul tip is considered a foul ball.

      A. True
      B. False

4:

```
Balls     1
Strikes   1
Outs      1
```

Runner on 1st

On the next pitch, R1 is stealing. Batter hits a foul tip that is missed (not caught) by the catcher. Catcher makes no attempt to throw out the runner. R1 must return to first because the foul tip is considered a foul ball.

      A. True
      B. False

<u>**5:**</u>

```
Balls      3
Strikes    1
Outs       1
```

Runner on 1st

On the next pitch, R1 is stealing. Batter takes ball 4. R1 slides into 2nd base, but over slides the base. Shortstop takes the throw from the catcher, and touches 2nd base (but does not tag R1) before R1 can get back to the base. What is the call?

   A. R1 is safe because he is entitled to 2nd base because of ball 4 on batter. The fact he over slid the base is irrelevant.
   B. R1 is no longer entitled to 2nd base because he touched the base and then went past it, and he is out because it is now a force play for him getting back to 2nd.
   C. R1 is no longer entitled to 2nd base because he touched the base and then went past it, but he is safe because it is not a force play and no tag was applied.

<u>**6:**</u>

```
Balls      1
Strikes    2
Outs       2
```

Runner on 3rd

On the next pitch, the batter hits a ground ball to shortstop and beats the throw to first base by a step. R3 crosses home plate. Batter-runner, thinking the first baseman has missed the ball, takes a couple of steps toward second. First baseman tags batter-runner coming back into 1st base. Batter-runner is correctly called out because he briefly attempted to advance to 2nd base. The run does not count because the batter-runner made the 3rd out at 1st base.

   A. True
   B. False

7: Runner attempting to score over slides home plate, and never touches it. He returns to his dugout believing he has scored.

   A. Catcher must tag the runner for him to be out even if it means following him into the dugout.
   B. Catcher must only step on home plate with possession of the ball for the runner to be out (and indicate he is making an appeal to the umpire).
   C. Runner is out as soon as he leaves the playing field. No need for the catcher to make a tag or step on home plate with the ball in his possession.

5.09(c) Appeal Plays

1:

Balls	1
Strikes	2
Outs	0

Bases empty

On the next pitch, the batter hits a home run. He misses 1st base on his trot around the bases. He realizes his mistake half way between 2nd and 3rd base, retouches 2nd base and then touches 1st base. He completes his trot by touching 2nd, 3rd, and home.

   A. Batter-runner's actions were legal, and his home run counts even if defensive team appeals he missed first base.
   B. Batter can not legally touch first base after he has reached 2nd base. Batter is out on appeal by the defensive team.

2: Two outs. Runner 1 and Runner 2 arrive at home at almost the same time. Runner 1 misses home and a split second later Runner 2 touches home. Runner 1 realizes he missed home, and tries to dive back but is tagged out before he can touch home. Even though Runner 1 made the third out, he was tagged out after Runner 2 crossed home plate, so Runner 2's run counts.

   A. True
   B. False

3: Pitcher attempts to make an appeal play to 1st base, but makes a wild throw that goes out of play into the stands.

> A. Considered to be a "no play". Pitcher can attempt a 2nd appeal before his next pitch to the plate.
> B. The pitcher is not allowed to make another appeal attempt to the same base.

5.10 Substitutions and Pitching Changes *(including visits to the mound).*

1: Which of the following statements is true:

> A. A pitcher may never change to another position during the game.
> B. A pitcher may change to another position only once during the same inning.
> C. A pitcher may change to another position an unlimited number of times.

2: Manager makes a visit to the mound to talk to his pitcher. Which of the following is true.

> A. Manager and any other coach is not allowed a second visit for the same batter during the same inning.
> B. Manager is not allowed a second visit for the same batter during the same inning, but another coach (for example, pitching coach) is allowed such a visit.
> C. Manager is allowed a visit for the same batter during the same inning, but he must remove the pitcher from the game.
> D. Manager is allowed a visit for the same batter during the same inning, and he does not have to remove the pitcher from the game.

3: Manager makes a visit to the mound to talk to his pitcher. After the visit, a pinch-hitter is sent into the game for the batter. Which of the following is true.

    A. Manager and any other coach is not allowed a visit to the mound for the pinch-hitter.
    B. Manager is allowed a visit for the pinch-hitter, but he must remove the pitcher from the game.
    C. Manager is allowed a visit for the pinch-hitter, and he does not have to remove the pitcher from the game.

4: In Major League baseball, mound visits without a pitching change are limited to _____ per team, per nine innings.

    A. 4
    B. 5
    C. 6
    D. 7

5: Pitcher for Team A is facing his second batter. Team A has exhausted its mound visits. Manager of Team A crosses the foul line on his way to the mound.

    A. Pitcher must be removed from the game.
    B. Pitcher must pitch to the current batter, then be removed from the game.
    C. Pitcher must pitch to the current batter and the next batter even if the current batter makes the third out of the inning and the next batter is the lead off hitter for the next inning.
    D. Pitcher must pitch to the current batter and must pitch to the next batter unless the current batter makes the third out of the inning.

5.11 Designated Hitter Rule

1: The Designated Hitter named in the starting lineup must come to bat at least one time, unless he is injured or the opposing club changes pitchers.

    A. True
    B. False

2: Second baseman is leading off and the Designated Hitter (DH) is batting fourth in their team's lineup. In the 4th inning, the DH enters the game to play second base. Which is true?

    A. Previous DH will continue to bat fourth, and the pitcher will bat in the lead off position.
    B. Previous DH will now bat in the lead off position, and the pitcher will bat in the fourth position.
    C. Previous DH will now bat in the lead off position, and a new DH can be inserted into the fourth position.

3: Which of the following statements is true?

    A. The game pitcher may only pinch-hit or pitch-run for the Designated Hitter.
    B. The game pitcher may pinch-hit for anyone in the line-up.
    C. The game pitcher can not pinch-hit or pitch-run for anyone.

4: Manager of Team A (home team) lists 10 players in his team's lineup card, but fails to indicate one as the Designated Hitter (DH). Manager of Team B brings the failure to list a DH to the attention of the umpire-in-chief before the start of the bottom of the 1st inning (i.e, after Team A has taken the field on defense but before they come to bat). Which of the following is the correct statement?

A. The listed player from Team A that did not assume a position on defense can remain in the game as the DH.
B. The pitcher for Team A will be required to bat in the batter order in place of the listed player from Team A that did assume a position on defense.
C. The pitcher for Team A will be required to bat and the Manager of Team A can choose where to insert him in the batting order.
D. The pitcher for Team A will be required to bat and the Manager of Team B can choose where to insert him in Team A's batting order.

5: Manager of Team A (visiting team) lists 10 players in his team's lineup card, but fails to indicate one as the Designated Hitter (DH). Manager of Team B brings the failure to list a DH to the attention of the umpire-in-chief before the start of the bottom of the 1st inning (i.e, after Team A has batted, but before they have taken the field on defense). Which of the following is the correct statement?

A. The DH can remain in the game, and can be any listed player that did not bat in the top of the first inning.
B. The DH can remain in the game, and can be any listed player even if they already batted in the top of the first inning.
C. The pitcher for Team A will be required to bat and the Manager of Team A can choose where to insert him in the batting order.
D. The pitcher for Team A will be required to bat and the Manager of Team B can choose where to insert him in Team A's batting order.

6: If a player on defense goes to the mound (replaces the pitcher), the move will terminate the Designated Hitter position for that club for the remainder of the game.

A. True
B. False

<u>7:</u> If a pitcher is batting for himself and is properly listed as both the pitcher and DH in the starting lineup:

      A. He may not continue as DH after he is removed as pitcher.
      B. He may continue as DH after he is removed as pitcher.

<u>8:</u> If a pitcher is batting for himself in the starting lineup (listed as both pitcher and DH on the lineup card), every subsequent pitcher must bat for himself as well.

      A. True
      B. Fals

5.12   Calling "Time" and Dead Balls

<u>1:</u> Batter hits a home run, but pulls a leg muscle and is unable to circle the bases. It is permissible to allow a pinch-runner to run out the home run.

      A. True
      B. False

<u>2:</u> If a fielder catches a fly ball then steps or falls into any out of play area:

      A. The ball is dead, time is called.
      B. The ball is live, time is not called.

<u>3:</u> After a dead ball, in order for the umpire to put the ball into play again:

      A. The pitcher must have possession of the baseball, but does not necessarily have to be on the pitcher's plate.
      B. The pitcher must have possession of the baseball, and has to be in contact with the pitcher's plate. The pitcher does not necessarily have to have possession of the baseball

6.00 Improper Play, Illegal Action, and Misconduct

6.01 Interference, Obstruction, and Catcher Collisions

6.01(a) Batter or Runner Interference

<u>1:</u>

```
Balls      1
Strikes    1
Outs       1

Runner on 3rd
```

On the next pitch, R3 attempts to steal home. The batter hinders the catcher in making the play at home.

      A. Batter is out, run counts.
      B. Runner is out, run does not count.

2:

```
Balls      1
Strikes    2
Outs       0
```

Runners on 1st and 3rd

On the next pitch, the batter hits a ground ball to 2nd base. R1 willfully interferes with the play at 2nd base with the intent to break up the double play. R3 crosses home plate.

    A. R1 is out for interference. R3 is also ruled out (run does not count), and the batter-runner is awarded 1st base.

    B. R1 is out for interference. The batter-runner is also ruled out. The run counts.

    C. R1 is out for interference. The batter-runner is also ruled out. The run does not count, R3 is returned to 3rd base.

3:

```
Balls      1
Strikes    1
Outs       0
```

Runners on 1st and 3rd

On the next pitch, the batter hits a dribbler in fair territory close to 1st base line. Catcher attempts to make a play on the ball, and the batter-runner willfully interferes with the catcher with the intent to break up a possible double play. R3 crosses home plate.

    A. Batter-runner is out for interference. R1 is also ruled out. The run counts.

    B. Batter-runner is out for interference. R1 is also ruled out. The run does not count, R3 is returned to 3rd base.

    C. Batter-runner is out for interference. R3 is also ruled out, run does not count. R1 is returned to 1st base.

4:

```
Balls      1
Strikes    2
Outs       0
```

Runner on 1st

On the next pitch, the batter hits a fair pop-up near 1st base. R1 unintentionally interferes with the 1st baseman attempting to catch the pop up, and the 1st baseman does not make the catch.

    A. The ball is live and in play since the interference was unintentional.
    B. The ball is dead. R1 is out for interference. The batter is also out.
    C. The ball is dead. R1 is out for interference. The batter is not out and returns to bat.
    D. The ball is dead. R1 is out for interference. The batter is awarded 1st base.

5: A runner who is adjudged to have hindered a fielder who is attempting to make a play on a batted ball is always ruled out even if the act is not intentional.

    A. True
    B. False

6:

```
Balls      2
Strikes    2
Outs       2
```

Runner on 1st

On the next pitch, the batter hits a foul pop up near first base. R1 interferes with the 1st baseman attempting to catch the ball, and is correctly declared out for the 3rd out of the inning.

    A. Same batter will lead off the next inning with a 2 ball, 2 strike count.
    B. Same batter will lead off the next inning with no count.
    C. Batter is considered to have completed his at-bat in this situation, and the first batter up the following inning will be the player who follows him in the batting order.

7: When a catcher and batter-runner going to first base have contact when the catcher is fielding the ball, there is generally no violation and nothing should be called.

      A. True
      B. False

8: If a runner that is in contact with a legally occupied base hinders a fielder in making a play, he is not considered to be out unless the hindrance is ruled to be intentional.

      A. True
      B. False

9:

```
Balls      1
Strikes    2
Outs       0
```

Runners on 2nd and 3rd

On the next pitch, the batter hits a ground ball to 3rd and R3 breaks for home. The 3rd baseman throws home and catches R3 in a run-down. R2 advances to 2nd base. In the run-down between 3rd and home, R3 unintentionally interferes with the 3rd baseman and is called out.

      A. R2 is also ruled out.
      B. R2 is not out, remains at 3rd base.
      C. R2 is not out, but is returned to 2nd base.

6.01(b) Fielder Right of Way

1: If a member of the team at bat (other than a runner) hinders a fielder's attempt to catch or field a *batted* ball, the ball is dead, the batter is declared out and all runners return to the bases occupied at the time of the pitch.

      A. True
      B. False

2: If a member of the team at bat (other than a runner) hinders a fielder's attempt to field a *thrown* ball, the ball is dead, the runner on whom the play is being made is declared out and all runners return to the last legally occupied base at the time of the interference.

      A. True
      B. False

6.01(c) Catcher Interference

1:

```
Balls      1
Strikes    2
Outs       1

Runner on 3rd
```

On the next pitch, the batter makes contact with the catcher's glove on his swing and catcher's interference is correctly called by the umpire. The batted ball ends up being a fly ball to the outfield that is caught by the right fielder. R3 tags up and crosses home plate.

    A. The ball is dead as soon as the catcher's interference is called. The batter is awarded 1st base and R3 must return to 3rd base, no run can score on this play.
    B. The batter is awarded 1st base on the play, and the run counts.
    C. Manager of the offense may elect to decline the interference call and accept the play resulting in the batter being out and the run counting.

2: If catcher's interference is called, the ball is immediately dead and no other play may progress.

      A. True
      B. False

6.01(d) Unintentional Interference

1: Batter hits a screaming ground ball past third base that is just fair. The ball is headed toward the bat-boy who is stationed in foul territory. Bat-boy realizes it is a fair ball and tries to get out of the way of the ball, but the ball strikes him.

      A. The ball is alive and in play since the interference by the bat-boy is ruled unintentional.
      B. The ball is dead and the umpire shall impose such penalties as in his opinion will nullify the act of interference.

2: Batter hits a screaming ground ball past third base that is just fair. The ball is headed toward the bat-boy who is stationed in foul territory. Bat-boy, thinking it is a foul ball, catches the ball then realizes his mistake and drops the ball on the ground.

      A. The ball is alive and in play since the interference by the bat-boy is ruled unintentional.
      B. The interference by the bat-boy is ruled intentional since he intentionally caught the ball. The ball is dead and the umpire shall impose such penalties as in his opinion will nullify the act of interference.

3: A bat-boy intentionally interferes with a fair batted ball. The ball is dead and:

      A. All runners advance two bases from the base that they legally occupied at the time of the pitch.
      B. All runners advance two bases from the base that they legally occupied at the time of the interference.
      C. The umpire shall impose such penalties as in his opinion will nullify the act of interference.

6.01(e) Spectator Interference

1: A spectator interferes with a thrown or batted ball. The ball should be ruled dead at the moment of interference and the umpire should impose such penalties as in his opinion will nullify the act of interference.

      A. True
      B. False

2:

Balls	1
Strikes	2
Outs	1

Runner on 3rd

On the next pitch, the batter hits a deep fly ball to the outfield. A spectator clearly interferes with the outfielder attempting to catch the fly ball.

      A. Batter is out for spectator interference. Runner remains on third base with two outs.
      B. Batter is out for spectator interference. The umpire may award the runner home if he believes the runner could have scored on a sacrifice fly.

6.01(g) Interference with squeeze play or steal of home

1:

```
Balls      2
Strikes    1
Outs       1
```

Runner on 3rd

Runner breaks for the plate on an attempted steal of home. Catcher, seeing the runner take off, steps in front of home plate before the pitch arrives then catches the pitch and tags the runner before he touches home.

    A. This is legal play by the catcher. Runner is out. Pitch is called a ball and the batter remains at bat with a 3 ball 1 strike count.
    B. Runner is awarded home (run scores). Pitch is called a ball and the batter remains at bat with a 3 ball 1 strike count.
    C. Interference is called on the catcher, resulting in the batter being awarded 1st base. Runner is out.
    D. Both a balk and interference is called on the play resulting in the run scoring and the batter being awarded 1st base.

6.01(h) Obstruction

1: _____ is the act of a fielder who, while not in possession of the ball and not in the act of fielding the ball, impedes the progress of any runner.

2: If a fielder commits obstruction on a runner but no play is being made on the runner, the ball is dead and all runners advance to the bases they would have reached, in the umpire's judgment, if there had been no obstruction.

    A. True
    B. False

3: If a fielder commits obstruction on the batter-runner before the batter-runner touches first base: the play shall proceed until no further action is possible, and the umpire will then call "time" and impose such penalties as in his judgment nullifies the act of obstruction.

    A. True
    B. False

6.01(i) Collisions at Home Plate

1: If a runner attempting to score deviates from his direct pathway to the plate in order to initiate contact with the catcher and then collides with the catcher.

    A. The ball is dead
    B. The runner is out.
    C. All other base runners are returned to the last base touched at the time of the collision.
    D. All of the above.
    E. None of the above.

2: The catcher may never block the pathway of a runner trying to score even if the catcher has possession of the ball.

    A. True
    B. False

3: Play at the plate, runner trying to score. Throw from the outfield bounces several feet from the plate and toward the 3rd base line. Catcher is trying to make a play on the ball and in doing so blocks the runner from reaching home. Runner is awarded home because the catcher blocked him from reaching it.

    A. True
    B. False

6.01(j) Sliding to bases on double play attempts

1: A "roll block" is considered to be a "bona fide slide" - a runner that uses a "roll block" for purposes of breaking up a double play can not be called out for interference.

  A. True
  B. False

6.02 Pitcher Illegal Action

6.02(a) Balks

1:

```
Balls      1
Strikes    2
Outs       2
```

Runners on 1st and 2nd

Pitcher delivers his next pitch without his pivot foot in contact with the pitcher's plate.

    A. Pitch is called a ball.
    B. Pitch is called a balk.
    C. Pitch is considered to be a "no pitch".

2:

```
Balls      1
Strikes    2
Outs       2
```

Bases empty

Pitcher delivers his next pitch without his pivot foot in contact with the pitcher's plate.

    A. Pitch is called a ball.
    B. Pitch is called a balk.
    C. Pitch is considered to be a "no pitch".

3:

```
Balls      1
Strikes    2
Outs       2
```

Runners on 1st and 2nd

Pitcher is called for a "quick pitch".

    A. Pitch is called a ball.
    B. Pitch is called a balk.
    C. Pitch is considered to be a "no pitch".

4:

```
Balls      1
Strikes    2
Outs       2
```

Bases empty

Pitcher is called for a "quick pitch".

    A. Pitch is called a ball.
    B. Pitch is called a balk.
    C. Pitch is considered to be a "no pitch".

5:

```
Balls       1
Strikes     2
Outs        2
```

Runners on 1st and 2nd

Pitcher, while touching the rubber, fakes a throw to *first base*. This is a balk.

    A. True
    B. False

6:

```
Balls       1
Strikes     2
Outs        2
```

Runners on 1st and 2nd

Pitcher, while touching the rubber, fakes a throw to *second base*. This is a balk.

    A. True
    B. False

7:

```
Balls       1
Strikes     2
Outs        2
```

Bases loaded

Pitcher, while touching the rubber, fakes a throw to third base. This is a balk.

    A. True
    B. False

8:

```
Balls      1
Strikes    1
Outs       0
```

Runners on 1st and 2nd

Pitcher comes to a set position, then the ball slips out of his hand and hits the ground. The pitch:

      A. Is ruled a balk.
      B. Is ruled a ball.
      C. Is ruled a "no pitch".

9:

```
Balls      1
Strikes    1
Outs       0
```

Runner on 1st

Pitcher commits a balk on the next pitch, follows through with the pitch and the batter slaps it for a clean single to right field. R1 reaches 2nd base safely.

      A. Balk overrules the base hit. R1 is awarded 2nd base. Batter returns to bat.
      B. Balk overrules the base hit. Since R1 reached 2nd base, he is now awarded 3rd base. Batter returns to bat.
      C. The play overrules the balk. Batter remains at 1st and R1 remains at second as if the balk never occurred.

10: The purpose of the balk rule is to prevent the pitcher from deliberately deceiving
_____ .

      A. The base runner only.
      B. The hitter only.
      C. Both the base runner and the hitter.

11: Team A is attempting to pull off the old "hidden ball trick". 1st baseman "secretly" has the ball in his possession. The pitcher steps on the rubber without the ball.

      A. This is a legal play.
      B. This is a balk.

12:

```
Balls       1
Strikes     2
Outs        0
```

Runner on 1st

Pitcher takes one hand off the ball while he is still in the set position. This is a balk.

    A. True
    B. False

13:

```
Balls       1
Strikes     2
Outs        0
```

Runners on 1st and 3rd

From the set position, the pitcher steps toward 3rd base without throwing, then throws to 1st base to attempt to pick off the runner. This is a balk.

    A. True
    B. False

14:

```
Balls       1
Strikes     2
Outs        0
```

Runner on 3rd

Pitcher changes from the set position to the wind-up position without disengaging the pitcher's plate. This is a balk.

    A. True
    B. False

6.02(b) Illegal pitches with bases unoccupied

1: Bases empty, 2 outs. Ball slips out of the pitcher's hand but does not cross the foul line.

    A. Is called a "no pitch".
    B. Is called a balk.
    C. Is called a ball.

2: Bases empty, 2 outs. Ball slips out of the pitcher's hand and crosses the foul line.

    A. Is called a "no pitch".
    B. Is called a balk.
    C. Is called a ball.

3: Runner on 1st, 2 outs. Ball slips out of the pitcher's hand but does not cross the foul line.

    A. Is called a "no pitch".
    B. Is called a balk.
    C. Is called a ball.

4: Runner on 1st, 2 outs. Ball slips out of the pitcher's hand and crosses the foul line.

    A. Is called a "no pitch".
    B. Is called a balk.
    C. Is called a ball.

5: If a pitcher makes an illegal pitch with the bases unoccupied, it is a:

    A. Ball.
    B. Balk.
    C. No pitch.

6.03 Batter Illegal Action

6.03(a) Batter out for Illegal Action

1: Batter hits a pitch fair while he has one foot on the ground entirely outside the batter's box:

   A. Is ruled a foul ball.
   B. Is in play (must have both feet out of the box to be penalized).
   C. Batter is out.

2: Pitcher is in the set position. Batter changes batter's boxes - going from hitting left-handed to right-handed before pitch is delivered.

   A. This is legal move by batter.
   B. Strike is called on the batter.
   C. Batter is out.

3: Runner on 1st, no outs. Left-handed batter at the plate. Catcher attempts to pick runner off 1st base. Batter steps out of the batter's box and interferes with the catcher's attempt at the pick off.

   A. Batter is ruled out.
   B. Runner is ruled out.
   C. Both the batter and runner are ruled out.

4: Runner on 1st, no outs. Left-handed batter at the plate. Catcher attempts to pick runner off 1st base. Batter steps out of the batter's box and interferes with the catcher's attempt at the pick off. Catcher recovers from the interference and throws out the runner at 1st. Batter is still out for his interference resulting in a double play.

   A. True
   B. False

5: Batter swings and makes contact with the pitch while half of his lead foot is outside the batter's box. He is out.

    A. True
    B. False

6: Batter hits a pitch foul while he has one foot on the ground entirely outside the batter's box. The batter is out.

    A. True
    B. False

6.03(b) Batting Out of Turn

1: Batter B bats out of order in Batter A's spot in the batting order. Batter B takes two strikes, and the defensive team then protests that Batter B is batting out of order.

    A. Batter B is out. Batter A comes to bat.
    B. Batter A is ruled out. Batter following Batter A in batting order comes to bat.
    C. No out. Batter A comes to bat with 0 ball 2 strike count.

2: Batter B bats out of order in Batter A's spot in the batting order. Batter B slaps a single to center field. The defensive team appeals to the umpire before the next pitch is made that Batter B was out of order.

    A. The play stands because the defensive team did not appeal before the at-bat was completed.
    B. Batter B is out. Batter A comes to bat.
    C. Batter A is ruled out. Batter following Batter A in batting order comes to bat.

3: Batter B bats out of order in Batter A's spot in the batting order. Batter B slaps a single to center field. Defense does not realize Batter B is out of order and the pitcher makes a pitch to the next batter. Who is now the legal batter?

      A. Batter A.
      B. Batter following Batter A in the lineup.
      C. Batter following Batter B in the lineup.

4: Runner on 1st, no outs. Batter B bats out of order in Batter A's spot in the batting order. Runner steals 2nd on the first pitch to Batter B (a strike taken by the batter). Batter B swings and misses on the next pitch. Defense then realizes Batter B is out of order and protests.

      A. Batter B is out, runner is returned to 1st base. Batter A comes to bat.
      B. Batter A is out, runner is returned to 1st base. Batter following Batter A in order comes to bat.
      C. No out. Batter A comes to bat with a 0 ball 2 strike count. Runner is returned to 1st base.
      D. No out. Batter A comes to bat with a 0 ball 2 strike count. Runner remains at 2nd base.

5: If the umpire notices a batter is batting out of order before either team brings attention to it, he should immediately call time and enforce the proper penalty for a player batting out of turn.

      A. True
      B. False

6: When a player bats out of turn (an improper batter), and a legal appeal is made by the defensive team:

      A. The proper batter is called out.
      B. The improper batter is called out.

7.00 Ending the Game

7.01 Regulation Games

1: A game is called in the bottom of the 4th inning because of rain with the home team ahead. This is a regulation game.

- A. True
- B. False

2: A game is called in the bottom of the 5th inning because of rain with the home team ahead. This is a regulation game.

- A. True
- B. False

3: A game is called in the bottom of the 5th inning because of rain with the visiting team ahead. This is a regulation game.

- A. True
- B. False

4: For an extra inning game, a runner will be placed on 2nd base to begin the inning for both teams starting in what inning (assuming 9 inning regulation game)?

    A. 10th inning.
    B. 11th inning.
    C. 12th inning.

5: What player is placed on 2nd base to begin the inning in an extra inning game?

    A. The player due up first in the inning (in essence, the leadoff hitter receives a free pass to 2nd base).
    B. The player immediately preceding the leadoff hitter in the order (for example, if clean-up hitter is leading off the inning, 3rd place hitter in lineup becomes runner at 2nd).
    C. A bench player who has not entered the game yet, and they will be the runner for every inning after that unless they get hurt (in essence, an "extra-inning designated runner").

6: If the umpire notices an improper runner is placed on 2nd base in an extra-inning game before either team brings attention to it, he should immediately bring attention to it and have the correct runner placed on base.

    A. True
    B. False

7: A runner is placed on 2nd base to begin the top of the 10th inning. Batter hits first pitch for a single, and the runner from 2nd scores. Defensive correctly points out that incorrect runner was placed on 2nd base:

    A. The run does not count. Correct runner is placed on 2nd, and no out is recorded.
    B. The run does not count. 1 out is recorded for the "illegal" runner.
    C. The run does not count. No out is recorded for the "illegal" runner (in essence, the offensive team forfeited their ghost runner by having an incorrect runner enter the game).
    D. The run counts. Play continues with a runner on 1st base and no outs.

7.02 Suspended, Postponed, and Tie Games

1:   Game is called in the bottom of the 3rd inning because of a *light failure* with the home team ahead. This becomes a suspended game.

      A. True
      B. False

2:   Game is called in the bottom of the 3rd inning because of a *local curfew* with the home team ahead. This becomes a suspended game.

      A. True
      B. False

3:   Game is called in the bottom of the 3rd inning because of *rain* with the home team ahead. This becomes a suspended game.

      A. True
      B. False

4:   Game is called in the top of the 6th inning because of *rain* with the score tied. This becomes a suspended game.

      A. True
      B. False

8.00 The Umpire

8.01 Umpire Qualifications and Authority

1: Batter hits a screaming line drive down the 3rd base line. Base umpire rules it a fair ball. 3rd Baseman argues with the call, and is immediately ejected by the umpire. At the moment of the ejection, the ball is dead and all runners advance to the bases they would have reached, in the umpire's judgment, if the play was allowed to continue.

       A. True
       B. False

8.02 Appeal of Umpire Decisions

1: Batter attempts to check his swing on a pitch outside the strike zone. Home plate umpire rules that he swung at the pitch. An appeal may be made that he did not swing.

    A. True
    B. False

2: Batter attempts to check his swing on a pitch outside the strike zone. Home plate umpire rules that he did not swing at the pitch. An appeal may be made to the base umpire that the batter swung.

    A. True
    B. False

2023 Rule Changes not incorporated into a specific section

1: The pitch clock begins to count down for the pitcher when:

    A. Pitcher receives the ball.
    B. Pitcher steps on the rubber.

2: With the bases empty, the pitch clock starts at _____ seconds.

    A. 10
    B. 15
    C. 20

3: With runners on base, the pitch clock starts at _____ seconds.

    A. 10
    B. 15
    C. 20

4: Batters must be in the batter's box and alert to the pitcher by the _____ -second mark on the pitch clock.

    A. 6
    B. 8
    C. 10

5: Pitchers are allowed _____ step-offs and/or pick-off attempts per plate appearance.

    A. 2
    B. 3
    C. 4

6: If pitcher exceeds his pick-off attempt limit for a particular runner, and does not pick off the runner on the play:

      A. A ball is added to the batter's count.
      B. A balk is called on the pitcher.

7: If pitcher exceeds his pick-off attempt limit for a particular runner, but picks off the runner on the play:

      A. A ball is added to the batter's count.
      B. A balk is called on the pitcher.
      C. No infraction is called.

8: Runner on 1st. Pitcher uses his maximum pick-off attempts for R1. R1 steals 2nd base. Pitcher is not allowed any pick-off attempts for the runner now on 2nd base.

      A. True
      B. False

Answers:

2.00 The Playing Field

1. The infield is a _90_ foot square

2. Any playing field constructed by a professional club after June 1, 1958 shall provide a minimum distance of _325_ feet from home base to the nearest fence, stand or other obstruction on the right and left field foul lines.

3. Any playing field constructed by a professional club after June 1, 1958 shall provide a minimum distance of **400** feet to the center field fence.

4. Home base is a _17_ inch square.

5. Beginning in 2023, the bases are an _18_ inch square. Previously, it was a 15 inch square for the bases.

6. The pitcher's plate is **24** inches by 6 inches

3.00 Equipment and Uniform

1. If a player intentionally discolors or damages the ball by rubbing it with soil, rosin, sand-paper, etc the player will be rejected from the game and automatically suspended for _**10**_ games.

2. The bat may not be covered for more than **18** inches from its end with any substance to improve the grip (i.e. pine tar).

3. True or False: If a player is discovered to be using a bat with pine tar above the legal limit, the batter is automatically out and ejected from the game.

    This is False.

    If an umpire discovers a batter is using a bat with pine tar above the legal limit, this will *not* be grounds for declaring the batter out, or ejecting from the game. The batter will simply be ordered to use a different bat.

4. A catcher may not use a mitt that is more than _**38**_ inches in circumference.

5. A first baseman may not use a glove that is more than _**13**_ inches long from top to bottom.

6. True or False: All players in both the Major Leagues and Minor Leagues must wear a double ear flap helmet while at bat.

    This is False.

    Only Minor League players must wear a double ear flap helmet.

7. True or False: All base coaches in both the Major Leagues and Minor Leagues must wear a protective helmet.

   This is True.

4.00 Game Preliminaries

4.03 Exchange of Lineup Cards

1. From Opening day through August 31 of the championship season and during postseason games, Major League Clubs may designate a maximum of **13** pitchers for a game.

2. From September 1 through the end of the championship season (including any tiebreaker games), Major League Clubs may designate a maximum of **14** pitchers for a game.

3. True or False: Players who qualify as "Two-Way Players" under Major League Rule 2(b)(2) may appear as pitchers during a game without counting toward a club's pitcher limitations.

   This is True.

4. A position player (a player not designated as a pitcher or two-way player on the lineup card) may come into pitch for his team if his team is losing by **8** runs or more or in extra innings.

5. A position player (a player not designated as a pitcher or two-way player on the lineup card) may come into pitch for his team if his team is winning by **10** runs or more in the 9th inning.

6. The **Umpire-in-chief** shall make certain that the original and copies of the respective batting orders are identical.

7. Unless the home club has given previous notice that the game has been postponed or will be delayed in starting, the umpires shall enter the playing field **five (5)** minutes before the hour set for the game to begin and proceed directly to home base where they shall be met by the managers of the opposing teams.

8. At the pre-game home plate meeting between umpires and managers, the **home team** manager (or his designee) shall give his batting order to the umpire-in-chief first.

9. True or False: Lineup cards presented to the umpire-in-chief by a manager in the pre-game meeting must list the fielding positions to be played by each player in the batting order.

This is False.

The lineup card should list the fielding positions to be played by each player in the batting order as a courtesy, but is not required.

10. True or False: Lineup cards presented to the umpire-in-chief by a manager in the pre-game meeting should not list a designated hitter that is in the starting lineup since there is no applicable fielding position for them.

This is False.

If a designated hitter (DH) is to be used, the lineup should list who the DH is.

11. True or False: Failure to list a potential substitute player in the lineup card presented to the umpire-in-chief by a manager in the pre-game meeting makes such potential substitute player ineligible to enter the game.

This is False.

As a courtesy, potential substitute players should be listed in the lineup card, but the failure to list a potential substitute player shall *not* make such player ineligible to enter the game.

12. The umpire-in-chief gains sole authority to determine when the game shall be called, suspended or resumed on account of weather or the condition of the playing field **when the home team's batting order is handed to him** at the pregame plate meeting.

13. The umpire-in-chief shall not call the game until at least **30** minutes after he has suspended play.

4.04 Weather and Field Conditions

1. Before the exchange of lineup cards, the **home team** shall be the sole judge as to whether a game shall not be started because of unsuitable weather conditions or the unfit conditions of the playing field, except for the second game of a conventional or split doubleheader.

2. The **Umpire-in-Chief of the first game** shall be the sole judge as to whether the second game of a conventional or split doubleheader shall not be started because of unsuitable weather conditions or the unfit conditions of the playing field.

4.08 Doubleheaders

1. The second game of a doubleheader shall start **30** minutes after the first game is completed, unless a longer interval (not to exceed **45** minutes) is declared by the umpire-in-chief and announced to the opposing managers at end of the first game.

2. True or False: When a rescheduled game is part of a doubleheader, the rescheduled game shall be the first game, and the second game shall be the regularly scheduled game for that date.

   This is False

   Correct answer is when a rescheduled game is part of a doubleheader, the **regularly scheduled game shall be the first game**, and the second game shall be the rescheduled game for that date.

5.00 - Playing the Game

5.02: Fielding positions

1. When a pitcher begins his delivery of the ball to the batter, the defensive team must have a minimum of **4** players (in addition to pitcher and catcher) with both feet completely in front of the outer boundary of the infield dirt.

2. The pitcher begins his motion to the plate when there are 3 infielders on the left side of the infield and an "illegal shift" is called. The batter does not swing at the pitch.

   Pitch is automatically called a "ball".

   If the defensive team is called for an "illegal shift", the pitch is called a "ball" and the ball is dead unless the batter reaches first base on a hit, an error, a base on balls, a hit batter, or otherwise, and all other runners advance at least one base. If this is the case, the play stands as if the violation never occurred. In addition, if any other play follows the violation (for example, sacrifice fly or sacrifice bunt), the manager of the offensive team may decline the penalty and accept the play.

3.

   ```
   Balls      1
   Strikes    2
   Outs       1

   Runner on 3rd
   ```

   The pitcher begins his motion to the plate when there are 3 infielders on the left side of the infield and an "illegal shift" is called. The batter swings at the pitch anyway and hits a fly ball to the outfield that is caught by the right fielder. R3 tags up and crosses home plate.

   Manager of the offense may elect to decline the "illegal shift" call and accept the play resulting in the batter being out and the run counting.

   See explanation to previous question.

5.05: When the Batter Becomes a Runner

1. A pitch bounces in front of home plate, then is hit fair by the batter.

   This is a fair ball and the batter becomes a runner.

2.
```
Balls      2
Strikes    2
Outs       1
```

   Runners on 1st and 2nd

   Next pitch is a swinging strike on the batter that is not caught by the catcher. Batter may attempt to advance to 1st base.

   This is False.

   The batter may not attempt to advance to 1st base on a dropped third strike when *1st base is occupied and there are less than 2 outs*.

3.
```
Balls      2
Strikes    2
Outs       2
```

   Runners on 1st and 2nd

   Next pitch is a called strike and is not caught by the catcher. Batter may attempt to advance to 1st base.

   This is True.

   The batter may attempt to advance to 1st base on a dropped third strike **when there are two outs** even if 1st base is occupied.

4.

```
Balls      2
Strikes    2
Outs       0
```

Runners on 2nd and 3rd

Next pitch is a swinging strike that is not caught by the catcher. Batter may attempt to advance to 1st base.

This is True.

The batter may attempt to advance to 1st base on a dropped third strike *when 1st base is not occupied*.

5.

```
Balls      2
Strikes    2
Outs       0
```

No Runners on base

Next pitch is a called strike on the batter that is not caught by the catcher. Batter may attempt to advance to 1st base.

This is True.

The batter may attempt to advance to 1st base on a dropped third strike *when 1st base is not occupied*.

---

6. The only time a batter may attempt to advance to 1st base when a third strike is not caught by the catcher is when there are two outs.

   This is False.

   The batter may attempt to advance to 1st base on a dropped third strike **when 1st base is not occupied even if there are less than two outs**.

7. If a pitch touches the ground, then hits the batter:

   Batter is awarded first base.

8. Batter hits a fair ball through the infield past the 2nd baseman and the ball subsequently hits the umpire stationed in shallow outfield:

   Batter becomes a runner, and may advance as many bases as possible.

   On this play, the batted ball had passed a fielder (the 2nd baseman) before it hit the umpire. Therefore, it is a live ball as if the umpire had not been hit.

9. If a fair fly ball is deflected by a fielder into the stands, or over the fence into *foul* territory:

   Batter is entitled to advance to second base.

10. If a fair fly ball is deflected by a fielder into the stands, or over the fence into *fair* territory:

    Batter is entitled to a home run.

5.06 Running the Bases

5.06(b) Advancing Bases

1.

Balls	2
Strikes	2
Outs	0

Runners on 1st and 2nd

On the next pitch, the batter hits a clean single to center field. R2, thinking the ball is going to be caught, never leaves 2nd base. R1 reaches 2nd base before the ball is returned to the infield. At this point both R1 and R2 are standing on 2nd base. Shortstop tags both R1 and R2. Who is out?

R2 is out.

R1 is forced to 2nd base, therefore he is the one with legal right to the base and ruled safe on this play. R2 is out.

2.

Balls	2
Strikes	2
Outs	0

Runner on 2nd

Batter hits a deep fly ball to center field that falls in for a hit. R2, thinking the ball is going to be caught, never leaves 2nd base. Batter-runner reaches 2nd base before the ball is returned to the infield. At this point both R2 and the batter-runner are standing on 2nd base. Shortstop tags both R1 and R2. Who is out?

Batter-runner is out.

Batter-runner is not forced to 2nd base (and R2 is legally occupying the base) therefore batter-runner is the one that is out.

3.

```
Balls      3
Strikes    2
Outs       2
```

Bases loaded

On the next pitch, the batter takes Ball 4. R2 is overzealous and runs past third base toward home and is tagged out on a throw by the catcher before R3 reaches home plate (R3 does touch home).

The run counts.

This is one is a little illogical base on most other rules - the rule here states the run counts based on the theory that the run was forced home by the base on balls and all that R3 needed to do was touch home (irregardless if R2 was out before he did so).

4. First baseman catches a fly pop near the dugout then falls into the dugout (dugout is considered out of play).

All runners advance one base.

5.

```
Balls      3
Strikes    2
Outs       0
```

Runner on 1st

On the next pitch, R1 is attempting to steal. Batter takes ball four, and the pitch gets by the catcher. R1 heads to 3rd, but misses 2nd base. R1 realizes he missed 2nd, and tries to get back to 2nd. Catcher throws ball to 2nd baseman who touches 2nd base before R1 gets back to 2nd (but does not tag R1).

R1 is out.

R1 was entitled to 2nd base, but **missed 2nd base** before he attempted to advance to 3rd base. Therefore, it basically becomes a **force play** for him to get back to 2nd base. The fielder can either tag the runner or **tag the base** to make the out.

6.

```
Balls      3
Strikes    2
Outs       0
```

Bases loaded

On the next pitch, the batter hits a fly ball in fair territory and the right fielder deliberately throws his glove at the ball and hits the ball while in flight.

Ball is live, all runners advance 3 bases (i.e, 3 runs score), batter-runner may advance to home base at his peril.

7.

```
Balls      3
Strikes    2
Outs       0
```

Runner on 1st

On the next pitch, R1 is stealing. Batter hits a slow roller down 3rd base line. R1 is past 2nd base and heading to 3rd when the 3rd baseman fields the ball and immediately throws to 1st base (makes the throw before the batter-runner reaches 1st base). The throw is wild and bounces out of play into the stands.

R1 is awarded 3rd base.

The wild throw by the 3rd baseman is considered to be the ***first play by an infielder***, therefore the award is 2 bases from the position of the runner ***at the time of the pitch***. The only exception is when all runners including the batter-runner have advanced at least one base, then the award is based on the position of the runner at the time of the throw.

8.

```
Balls      3
Strikes    2
Outs       0
```

Runner on 1st

R1 is stealing. Batter hits a slow roller down third base line. R1 is past 2nd base and heading to 3rd when the 3rd baseman fields the ball. The 3rd baseman takes a couple of steps toward R1 in an attempt to tag him. R1 stops, so the 3rd baseman throws to 1st base instead. The throw is wild and bounces out of play into the stands.

R1 is allowed to score.

The wild throw by the 3rd baseman is ***not*** considered to be the first play by an infielder. In this case "the couple of steps toward R1 in an attempt to tag him" is considered the "first play". Because it is not the first play by an infielder, the award is 2 bases from the position of the runner ***at the time of the throw***.

9.

```
Balls      3
Strikes    2
Outs       0
```

Runner on 1st

R1 is stealing. Batter slaps a base hit to center field. R1 is past 2nd base and heading to 3rd when the centerfielder fields the ball. The centerfielder immediately throws to 3rd base in an attempt to throw out R1. The throw is wild and bounces out of play into the stands.

R1 is allowed to score.

The wild throw by the centerfielder is **not** the first play by an **infielder**. Because it is not the first play by an infielder, the award is 2 bases from the position of the runner **at the time of the throw**.

10.

```
Balls      3
Strikes    2
Outs       0
```

Runner on 1st

While engaged with the pitcher's plate, the pitcher makes a legal pick off attempt at first base. The pick off attempt is wild and the ball bounces out of play into the stands.

R1 is awarded 2nd base.

It is a **one-base** award when the **pitcher** makes a wild throw out of play from his legal pitching position.

11.

```
Balls      3
Strikes    2
Outs       0
```

Runner on 3rd

On the next pitch, the batter hits a fly ball to the right fielder. Thinking the ball is not going to be caught, R3 breaks for home. Right fielder catches the ball and immediately throws to 3rd in an attempt to catch R3. The throw is wild and bounces out of play into the stands. R3 is awarded home on the wild throw. He touches home without ever returning to retouch 3rd base. Defense makes an appeal by throwing to 3rd, saying R3 did not tag up after the catch.

R3 is out.

Even though R3 was awarded home on the wild throw, he still must return and touch 3rd base because he did not tag-up on the original play. He may return to retouch 3rd base after the ball is dead as it would be in this situation.

12.

```
Balls      3
Strikes    2
Outs       0
```

Runner on 1st

Pitcher makes a legal pickoff attempt while engaged with the pitcher's plate, but throws wild and the ball goes out of play.

R1 is awarded 2nd base.

A wild throw out play by the pitcher while engaged with the pitcher's plate is a one base award.

13.

```
Balls       3
Strikes     2
Outs        0
```

Runner on 1st

Runner on 1st, no outs. Pitcher legally disengages the pitcher's plate and attempts to pick off the runner at 1st. The throw is wild and the ball goes out of play.

R1 is awarded 3rd base.

When a pitcher disengages the pitcher's plate, he becomes an infielder. A wild throw out of play by an infielder is a two base award.

14. Batter is hit with pitch outside the strike zone. The ball is dead, batter is awarded 1st base, and the base runners:

Advance one base only if forced to advance.

15. If a fielder deliberately throws his glove and touches a ***thrown ball***, it is:

Two base award.

16.

```
Balls       2
Strikes     1
Outs        1
```

Runner on 2nd

On the next pitch, the batter hits an infield pop that hits R2 while R2 is still standing on 2nd base (hits R2 before it has passed an infielder).

Batter hits an infield pop that hits R2 while R2 is still standing on 2nd base (hits R2 before it has passed an infielder).

R2 is out, the batter is awarded 1st base.

17.

```
Balls       2
Strikes     1
Outs        1
```

Runners on 1st and 2nd

On the next pitch, the batter hits a routine infield pop (infield fly is called) that hits R2 while *R2 is still standing on 2nd base.*

Batter is out (on infield fly call), R2 remains at 2nd.

18.

```
Balls       2
Strikes     1
Outs        1
```

Runners on 1st and 2nd

On the next pitch, the batter hits a routine infield pop (infield fly is called) that hits R2 while R2 *is off of 2nd base.*

Both runner and batter are out.

19.

```
Balls       2
Strikes     1
Outs        1
```

Runners on 1st and 2nd

On the next pitch, the batter hits a line drive toward the pitcher. Pitcher deflects the ball, the ball hits off of R2 a couple of steps off of 2nd base, and then is caught by the shortstop before the ball ever touches the ground.

No catch. Once the ball bounces off the runner it is treated as if it had touched the ground,

5.06(c) Dead Balls

1. True or False: If a fair ball touches an umpire before it has passed an infielder other than the pitcher, it is considered a dead ball and runners advance if forced.

   This is true.

2. If a fair ball touches an umpire after it has passed an infielder other than the pitcher, it is considered a dead ball and runners advance if forced.

   This is false.

   It is considered a live ball and in play.

3.
   ```
   Balls     2
   Strikes   2
   Outs      0
   ```

   Bases empty.

   Bases empty, no outs. Batter swings and misses at strike three. Pitch gets by the catcher, but rebounds off the umpire. Catcher catches the rebound before it hits the ground. Batter may attempt to advance to first base.

   This is true.

4.
```
Balls      2
Strikes    1
Outs       0

Runner on 1st
```

The next pitch gets past the catcher, and lodges in the umpire's mask.   Runner is awarded 2nd base.

This is true.

5.07 Pitching

5.07(a) Legal Pitching Delivery

1. There are two legal pitching positions, the windup position and the **set** position.

2. True or False: Pitchers can not take signs from the catcher while in contact with the pitcher's plate.

   This is false.

   It is actually where they have to take signs.

3. When a pitcher holds the ball with both hands in front of his body with his pivot foot in contact with the pitcher's plate and his other foot free, he is considered to be:

   In the set position.

4. In the windup position, a pitcher is not permitted to have both feet in contact with the pitcher's plate.

   This is false.

5. From the windup position, a pitcher may step and throw to a base in an attempt to pick-off a runner without committing a balk.

   This is true.

6. From the set position, a pitcher may legally disengage from the pitcher's plate by stepping backward or forward with his pivot foot.

   This is false.

   Pitchers may only disengage from the pitcher's plate by stepping **backward**.

7. From the set position, the pitcher is required to come to a complete stop after his stretch even if there are no runners on base.

   This is false.

5.07(d) Throwing to the Base

1. True or False: Runner on 1st. Pitcher, from set position, attempts to pick off runner with a snap throw followed by a step directly toward 1st base.   This is legal, and not a balk.

   This is false.

   The step toward 1st base must be *before* the throw.

2. True or False: If a pitcher, from the set position, removes his pivot foot from contact with the pitcher's plate by stepping backward with that foot, he is now considered to be an infielder.

   This is true.

3. An ambidextrous pitcher is allowed to switch pitching arms whenever he wants during a single at-bat to the same batter.

   This is false.

5.08 How a Team Scores

1.

```
Balls      2
Strikes    1
Outs       2
```

Bases Loaded

Batter hits a ground ball to deep third. Third baseman fields the ball and beats R2 to third for the force out. R3, with a huge jump, crosses home plate before the force play is made at third. The run counts.

This is false.

The third out recorded at third base **was a force out**, therefore the run does not count even though R3 crossed home before the out.

2.

```
Balls      2
Strikes    1
Outs       2
```

Runners on 2nd and 3rd

Batter hits a ground ball to deep third. Third baseman fields the ball and tags R2 coming into third base. R3, with a huge jump, crosses home plate before the tag is applied on R2 at third. The run counts.

This is true.

The third out recorded at third base **was not a force out**, therefore the run counts because R3 crossed home before the out.

3.

```
Balls      2
Strikes    1
Outs       2
```

Runner on 3rd

Batter hits a ground ball to deep short. Shortstop fields the ball and throws the batter out at first by half-step. R3, with a huge jump, crosses home plate before the play is made at first. The run counts.

This is false.

The third out was recorded on the batter-runner *before he reached first base safely*, therefore the run does not count even though R3 reached home before the out was recorded at 1st base.

4.

```
Balls      2
Strikes    1
Outs       1
```

Runners on 1st and 2nd

On the next pitch, the batter hits an inside the park home run. R2 misses third, and is called out on appeal. Two runs count.

This is true.

R2 is only the 2nd out of the inning, therefore the other two runs count. If R2 had been the 3rd out of the inning, no runs would count even though the appeal and out was recorded after the other two runners reached home.

5.

```
Balls      2
Strikes    1
Outs       2
```

Runners on 1st and 2nd

On the next pitch, the batter hits an inside the park home run. R2 misses third, and is called out on appeal. Two runs count.

This is false.

R2 is the 3rd out of the inning, so no runs count even though the appeal and out was recorded after the other two runners reached home.

6.

```
Balls      2
Strikes    1
Outs       2
```

Bases loaded

On the next pitch, the batter hits a grand slam home run. On appeal, the batter is declared out for missing first base. How many runs count.

No runs counts is the correct answer here.

Since the *batter-runner did not reach first base safely* and was the third out, no runs count.

5.09 Making an Out

5.09(a) Retiring the Batter

---

1. First baseman, on a foul pop near the dugout, reaches into the dugout (without stepping into it) to make the catch. The batter is out.

   This is true.

---

2. First baseman, on a foul pop near the dugout, has one foot on the ground in play and one foot over the inside of the dugout (but not touching the ground inside the dugout) when he makes the catch. Legal catch, batter is out.

   This is true.

---

3. Center fielder is racing back on a deep fly ball. He makes the catch and immediately runs into the fence which causes him to drop the ball. The batter is out.

   This is false.

   In this case, the fielder did not meet the requirements for a legal catch - his release of the ball was not voluntary and intentional.

---

4. To make a legal catch, the fielder must hold the ball long enough to prove that he has complete control of the ball and that his release of the ball is voluntary and **intentional**.

---

5. Center field and right fielder converge on a fly ball. Center fielder is first to touch the ball. He juggles the ball and drops it. Right fielder catches it before it hits the ground:

   This is a legal catch and the runners may leave their bases at the point the center fielder first touches the ball.

---

6. Right fielder is chasing down a foul ball near the stands. He hops on top of the tarp that is stored in play along the grandstand fence. He makes the catch while standing on top of the tarp with both feet. The batter is out.

This is true.

7. Right fielder is chasing down a foul ball near the stands. He reaches into the stands in an attempt to make the catch. A fan prevents him from making the catch. The batter is out on fan interference.

This is false.

A fielder can **reach into the stands** to make a legal catch but if a fan prevents him from making the catch it is **not considered fan interference**.

8. Right fielder is chasing down a foul ball near the stands. A fan reaches out over the playing field and prevents the right fielder from making the catch. The batter is out on fan interference.

This is true.

Since the fan reached out **over the playing field** to prevent the catch, this **is considered fan interference**.

9. No one on base. Two outs. Batter takes strike three. Catcher misses the catch, the ball hits his chest protector, and he traps it against his chest before the ball hits the ground:

Strike three - batter is out is the correct answer.

Catcher is considered to have "caught" the third strike even though he trapped the ball against his chest.

10. Batter hits a pitch. The ball bounces and hits him while he is still in the batter's box:

Foul ball is the correct answer here.

Since the batter **had NOT left the batter's box** when the batted ball hit him, it is a **foul ball**.

11. Batter hits a pitch. The ball bounces and hits him after he has left the batter's box.

Batter is out is the correct answer here.

Since the batter *had left the batter's box* when the batted ball hit him, *he is out*.

12. Batter hits a dribbler in fair territory. Batter drops his bat and the ball rolls against the bat in fair territory. There was no intention by the batter to interfere with the course of the ball. What is the call?:

Since there was no intention by the batter here, the ball is live and he may continue to advance around the bases.

13. Batter hits an infield pop-up and accidentally without any intent throws his bat on the swing. The thrown bat interferes with the infielder attempting to make the catch. What is the call?

Batter is out is the correct answer here.

Even though there was no intent by the batter to throw his bat, he is still out on this play.

14.

```
Balls      2
Strikes    1
Outs       1
```

Runners on 1st and 3rd

On the next pitch, the batter hits a pop up to 2nd baseman. The 2nd baseman intentionally drops the pop up (after making contact with the ball). What is the call?

Ball is dead - batter is out, runners are returned to 1st and 3rd.

Even though the infield fly rule is not in effect on this play, the fact the fielder intentionally dropped the ball *after making contact with the ball* makes this an illegal act by the fielder.

15.

```
Balls      2
Strikes    1
Outs       1
```

Runners on 1st and 3rd

On the next pitch, the batter hits a pop up to 2nd baseman. The 2nd baseman intentionally lets the pop-up drop without touching the ball before it hits the ground. What is the call?

Legal play - ball is live and in play.

Even though the fielder intentionally missed the ball, the fact *he never touched the ball before it hit the ground* makes it a legal play.

16.

```
Balls      1
Strikes    2
Outs       2
```

Runner on 3rd

On the next pitch, R3 attempts to steal home. The pitch hits R3 in the strike zone. What is the call?

Strike 3 on batter, 3 outs, run does not count.

17.

```
Balls      1
Strikes    2
Outs       1
```

Runner on 3rd

On the next pitch, R3 attempts to steal home. The pitch hits R3 in the strike zone. What is the call?

Strike 3 on batter, 2 outs, run counts.

5.09(b) Retiring a Runner

1. Bottom of ninth, scored tied. Runner on 1st, one out. Batter hits an apparent game winning home run. R1, thinking this automatically wins the game, cuts across the field toward his bench as the batter-runner circles the bases. What is the call?

   R1 is out for abandoning his effort to run the bases. Batter-runner run counts. Game over, the home team wins by one run.

2. If a runner falsely believes he is out on a close play at first base and starts for the dugout and progresses a reasonable distance, he will be declared out for abandoning the bases even if no tag is applied.

   This is True.

3.

```
Balls      1
Strikes    1
Outs       1
```

Runner on 1st

On the next pitch, R1 is stealing. Batter hits a foul tip that is caught by the catcher. Catcher makes no attempt to throw out the runner. R1 must return to first because the foul tip is considered a foul ball.

This is False.

Foul tip ***caught by the catcher*** is considered a ***strike***, not a foul ball. Runner does not have to return to 1st base.

4.

```
Balls      1
Strikes    1
Outs       1
```

Runner on 1st

On the next pitch, R1 is stealing. Batter hits a foul tip that is missed (not caught) by the catcher. Catcher makes no attempt to throw out the runner. R1 must return to first because the foul tip is considered a foul ball.

This is True.

Foul tip ***not caught by the catcher*** is considered a ***foul ball***. Runner must return to 1st base.

5.

```
Balls      3
Strikes    1
Outs       1
```

Runner on 1st

On the next pitch, R1 is stealing. Batter takes ball 4. R1 slides into 2nd base, but over slides the base. Shortstop takes the throw from the catcher, and touches 2nd base (but does not tag R1) before R1 can get back to the base. What is the call?

R1 is no longer entitled to 2nd base because he touched the base and then went past it, but he is safe because it is not a force play and no tag was applied.

6.

```
Balls      1
Strikes    2
Outs       2
```

Runner on 3rd

On the next pitch, the batter hits a ground ball to shortstop and beats the throw to first base by a step. R3 crosses home plate. Batter-runner, thinking the first baseman has missed the ball, takes a couple of steps toward second. First baseman tags batter-runner coming back into 1st base. Batter-runner is correctly called out because he briefly attempted to advance to 2nd base. The run does not count because the batter-runner made the 3rd out at 1st base.

This is False.

On this play, the batter-runner was *deemed to have reached 1st base safely*, and was put out on his attempt to advance to 2nd base. The run counts because R3 crossed home plate before the third out was made.

7. Runner attempting to score over slides home plate, and never touches it. He returns to his dugout believing he has scored.

Catcher must only step on home plate with possession of the ball for the runner to be out (and indicate he is making an appeal to the umpire).

5.09(c) Appeal Plays

1.

```
Balls      1
Strikes    2
Outs       0
```

Bases empty

On the next pitch, the batter hits a home run. He misses 1st base on his trot around the bases. He realizes his mistake half way between 2nd and 3rd base, retouches 2nd base and then touches 1st base. He completes his trot by touching 2nd, 3rd, and home.

Batter can not legally touch first base after he has reached 2nd base. Batter is out on appeal by the defensive team.

---

2. Two outs. Runner 1 and Runner 2 arrive at home at almost the same time. Runner 1 misses home and a split second later Runner 2 touches home. Runner 1 realizes he missed home, and tries to dive back but is tagged out before he can touch home. Even though Runner 1 made the third out, he was tagged out after Runner 2 crossed home plate, so Runner 2's run counts.

   This is False.

---

3. Pitcher attempts to make an appeal play to 1st base, but makes a wild throw that goes out of play into the stands.

   The pitcher is not allowed to make another appeal attempt to the same base.

5.10 Substitutions and Pitching Changes *(including visits to the mound).*

1. Which of the following statements is true:

   – A pitcher may never change to another position during the game.
   – A pitcher may change to another position only once during the same inning.
   – A pitcher may change to another position an unlimited number of times.

   Correct: A pitcher may change to another position only once during the same inning.

2. Manager makes a visit to the mound to talk to his pitcher.

   Manager and any other coach is not allowed a second visit for the same batter during the same inning

3. Manager makes a visit to the mound to talk to his pitcher. After the visit, a pinch-hitter is sent into the game for the batter. Which of the following is true.

   Manager is allowed a visit for the pinch-hitter, but he must remove the pitcher from the game.

4. In Major League baseball, mound visits without a pitching change are limited to **five (5)** per team, per nine innings.

5. Pitcher for Team A is facing his second batter. Team A has exhausted its mound visits. Manager of Team A crosses the foul line on his way to the mound.

   Pitcher must pitch to the current batter and must pitch to the next batter unless the current batter makes the third out of the inning.

5.11 Designated Hitter Rule

1. The Designated Hitter named in the starting lineup must come to bat at least one time, unless he is injured or the opposing club changes pitchers.

   This is True.

2. Second baseman is leading off and the Designated Hitter (DH) is batting fourth in their team's lineup. In the 4th inning, the DH enters the game to play second base.

   Previous DH will continue to bat fourth, and the pitcher will bat in the lead off position.

3. Which of the following statements is true?

   – The game pitcher may only pinch-hit or pitch-run for the Designated Hitter.
   – The game pitcher may pinch-hit for anyone in the line-up.
   – The game pitcher can not pinch-hit or pitch-run for anyone.

   Correct: The game pitcher may only pinch-hit or pitch-run for the Designated Hitter.

4. Manager of Team A (home team) lists 10 players in his team's lineup card, but fails to indicate one as the Designated Hitter (DH). Manager of Team B brings the failure to list a DH to the attention of the umpire-in-chief before the start of the bottom of the 1st inning (i.e, after Team A has taken the field on defense but before they come to bat).

   The pitcher for Team A will be required to bat in the batter order in place of the listed player from Team A that did assume a position on defense.

5. Manager of Team A (visiting team) lists 10 players in his team's lineup card, but fails to indicate one as the Designated Hitter (DH). Manager of Team B brings the failure to list a DH to the attention of the umpire-in-chief before the start of the bottom of the 1st inning (i.e, after Team A has batted, but before they have taken the field on defense).

   The pitcher for Team A will be required to bat and the Manager of Team A can choose where to insert him in the batting order.

6. If a player on defense goes to the mound (replaces the pitcher), the move will terminate the Designated Hitter position for that club for the remainder of the game.

   This is True.

7. If a pitcher is batting for himself and is properly listed as both the pitcher and DH in the starting lineup:

   He may continue as DH after he is removed as pitcher.

8. For 2022 season: If a pitcher is batting for himself in the starting lineup, every subsequent pitcher must bat for himself as well (i.e., No DH for remainder of game)

   This is False.

5.12 Calling "Time" and Dead Balls

---

1. Batter hits a home run, but pulls a leg muscle and is unable to circle the bases. It is permissible to allow a pinch-runner to run out the home run.

   This is True.

---

2. If a fielder catches a fly ball then steps or falls into any out of play area:

   The ball is dead, time is called.

---

3. After a dead ball, in order for the umpire to put the ball into play again:

   The pitcher must have possession of the baseball, and has to be in contact with the pitcher's plate.

6.00 Improper Play, Illegal Action, and Misconduct

6.01 Interference, Obstruction, and Catcher Collisions

6.01(a) Batter or Runner Interference

1.

```
Balls      1
Strikes    1
Outs       1
```

Runner on 3rd

On the next pitch, R3 attempts to steal home. The batter hinders the catcher in making the play at home.

Runner is out, run does not count.

2.

```
Balls      1
Strikes    2
Outs       0
```

Runners on 1st and 3rd

On the next pitch, the batter hits a ground ball to 2nd base. R1 willfully interferes with the play at 2nd base with the intent to break up the double play. R3 crosses home plate.

R1 is out for interference. The batter-runner is also ruled out. The run does not count, R3 is returned to 3rd base.

3.

```
Balls      1
Strikes    1
Outs       0
```

Runners on 1st and 3rd

On the next pitch, the batter hits a dribbler in fair territory close to 1st base line. Catcher attempts to make a play on the ball, and the batter-runner willfully interferes with the catcher with the intent to break up a possible double play. R3 crosses home plate.

Batter-runner is out for interference. R3 is also ruled out, run does not count. R1 is returned to 1st base.

4.

```
Balls      1
Strikes    2
Outs       0
```

Runner on 1st

On the next pitch, the batter hits a fair pop-up near 1st base. R1 unintentionally interferes with the 1st baseman attempting to catch the pop up, and the 1st baseman does not make the catch.

The ball is dead. R1 is out for interference. The batter is awarded 1st base.

5. A runner who is adjudged to have hindered a fielder who is attempting to make a play on a batted ball is always ruled out even if the act is not intentional.

This is True.

6.

```
Balls      2
Strikes    2
Outs       2
```

Runner on 1st

On the next pitch, the batter hits a foul pop up near first base. R1 interferes with the 1st baseman attempting to catch the ball, and is correctly declared out for the 3rd out of the inning.

Batter is considered to have completed his at-bat in this situation, and the first batter up the following inning will be the player who follows him in the batting order.

7. When a catcher and batter-runner going to first base have contact when the catcher is fielding the ball, there is generally no violation and nothing should be called.

   This is True.

8. If a runner that is in contact with a legally occupied base hinders a fielder in making a play, he is not considered to be out unless the hindrance is ruled to be intentional.

   This is True.

9.

```
Balls      1
Strikes    2
Outs       0
```

Runners on 2nd and 3rd

On the next pitch, the batter hits a ground ball to 3rd and R3 breaks for home. The 3rd baseman throws home and catches R3 in a run-down. R2 advances to 2nd base. In the run-down between 3rd and home, R3 unintentionally interferes with the 3rd baseman and is called out.

R2 is not out, but is returned to 2nd base.

6.01(b) Fielder Right of Way

1. True or False: If a member of the team at bat (other than a runner) hinders a fielder's attempt to catch or field a batted ball, the ball is dead, the batter is declared out and all runners return to the bases occupied at the time of the pitch.

    This is True.

2. True or False: If a member of the team at bat (other than a runner) hinders a fielder's attempt to field a thrown ball, the ball is dead, the runner on whom the play is being made is declared out and all runners return to the last legally occupied base at the time of the interference.

    This is True.

6.01(c) Catcher Interference

1. Runner on 3rd, one out. Batter makes contact with catcher's glove on his swing and catcher's interference is correctly called by the umpire. The batted ball ends up being a fly ball to the outfield that is caught by the right fielder. R3 tags up and crosses home plate.

    Manager of the offense may elect to decline the interference call and accept the play resulting in the batter being out and the run counting.

2. If catcher's interference is called, the ball is immediately dead and no other play may progress.

    This is False.

6.01(d) Unintentional Interference

1. Batter hits a screaming ground ball past third base that is just fair. The ball is headed toward the bat-boy who is stationed in foul territory. Bat-boy realizes it is a fair ball and tries to get out of the way of the ball, but the ball strikes him.

    The ball is alive and in play since the interference by the bat-boy is ruled unintentional.

2. Batter hits a screaming ground ball past third base that is just fair. The ball is headed toward the bat-boy who is stationed in foul territory. Bat-boy, thinking it is a foul ball, catches the ball then realizes his mistake and drops the ball on the ground.

    The interference by the bat-boy is ruled intentional since he intentionally caught the ball. The ball is dead and the umpire shall impose such penalties as in his opinion will nullify the act of interference.

3. A bat-boy intentionally interferes with a fair batted ball. The ball is dead and:

    The umpire shall impose such penalties as in his opinion will nullify the act of interference.

6.01(e) Spectator Interference

1. A spectator interferes with a thrown or batted ball. The ball should be ruled dead at the moment of interference and the umpire should impose such penalties as in his opinion will nullify the act of interference.

   This is True.

2.

   ```
   Balls      1
   Strikes    2
   Outs       1
   ```

   Runner on 3rd

   On the next pitch, the batter hits a deep fly ball to the outfield. A spectator clearly interferes with the outfielder attempting to catch the fly ball.

   Batter is out for spectator interference. The umpire may award the runner home if he believes the runner could have scored on a sacrifice fly.

6.01(g) Interference with squeeze play or steal of home

1.

   ```
   Balls      2
   Strikes    1
   Outs       1
   ```

   Runner on 3rd

   Runner breaks for the plate on an attempted steal of home. Catcher, seeing the runner take off, steps in front of home plate before the pitch arrives then catches the pitch and tags the runner before he touches home.

   Both a balk and interference is called on the play resulting in the run scoring and the batter being awarded 1st base.

6.01(h) Obstruction

1. **Obstruction** is the act of a fielder who, while not in possession of the ball and not in the act of fielding the ball, impedes the progress of any runner.

2. If a fielder commits obstruction on a runner but no play is being made on the runner, the ball is dead and all runners advance to the bases they would have reached, in the umpire's judgment, if there had been no obstruction.

   This is False.

3. If a fielder commits obstruction on the batter-runner before the batter-runner touches first base: the play shall proceed until no further action is possible, and the umpire will then call "time" and impose such penalties as in his judgment nullifies the act of obstruction.

   This is False.

6.01(i) Collisions at Home Plate

1. If a runner attempting to score deviates from his direct pathway to the plate in order to initiate contact with the catcher and then collides with the catcher.

   All of the following are true:

   – The ball is dead
   – The runner is out.
   – All other base runners are returned to the last base touched at the time of the collision.

2. True or False: The catcher may never block the pathway of a runner trying to score even if the catcher has possession of the ball.

   This is False.

3. Play at the plate, runner trying to score. Throw from the outfield bounces several feet from the plate and toward the 3rd base line. Catcher is trying to make a play on the ball and in doing so blocks the runner from reaching home. Runner is awarded home because the catcher blocked him from reaching it.

   This is False.

6.01(j) Sliding to bases on double play attempts

1. A "roll block" is considered to be a "bona fide slide" - a runner that uses a "roll block" for purposes of breaking up a double play can not be called out for interference.

   This is False.

6.02 Pitcher Illegal Action

6.02(a) Balks

1.
   ```
   Balls      1
   Strikes    2
   Outs       2
   ```

   Runners on 1st and 2nd

   Pitcher delivers his next pitch without his pivot foot in contact with the pitcher's plate.

   Pitch is called a balk.

2.

```
Balls      1
Strikes    2
Outs       2
```

Bases empty

Pitcher delivers his next pitch without his pivot foot in contact with the pitcher's plate.

Pitch is called a ball.

3.

```
Balls      1
Strikes    2
Outs       2
```

Runners on 1st and 2nd

Pitcher is called for a "quick pitch".

Pitch is called a balk.

4.

```
Balls      1
Strikes    2
Outs       2
```

Bases empty

Pitcher is called for a "quick pitch".

Pitch is called a ball.

5.

```
Balls      1
Strikes    2
Outs       2
```

Runners on 1st and 2nd

Pitcher, while touching the rubber, fakes a throw to *first base*. This is a balk.

This is True.

6.

```
Balls      1
Strikes    2
Outs       2
```

Runners on 1st and 2nd

Pitcher, while touching the rubber, fakes a throw to *second base*. This is a balk.

This is False.

7.

```
Balls      1
Strikes    2
Outs       2
```

Bases loaded

Pitcher, while touching the rubber, fakes a throw to third base. This is a balk.

This is True.

8.

```
Balls      1
Strikes    1
Outs       0
```

Runners on 1st and 2nd

Pitcher comes to a set position, then the ball slips out of his hand and hits the ground. The pitch:

Is ruled a balk.

9.

```
Balls      1
Strikes    1
Outs       0
```

Runner on 1st

Pitcher commits a balk on the next pitch, follows through with the pitch and the batter slaps it for a clean single to right field. R1 reaches 2nd base safely.

The play overrules the balk. Batter remains at 1st and R1 remains at second as if the balk never occurred.

10. The purpose of the balk rule is to prevent the pitcher from deliberately deceiving the **base runner only**.

11. Team A is attempting to pull off the old "hidden ball trick". 1st baseman "secretly" has the ball in his possession. The pitcher steps on the rubber without the ball.

This is a balk.

12.

```
Balls      1
Strikes    2
Outs       0
```

Runner on 1st

Pitcher takes one hand off the ball while he is still in the set position. This is a balk.

This is True.

13.

```
Balls      1
Strikes    2
Outs       0
```

Runners on 1st and 3rd

From the set position, the pitcher steps toward 3rd base without throwing, then throws to 1st base to attempt to pick off the runner. This is a balk.

This is True.

14.

```
Balls      1
Strikes    2
Outs       0
```

Runner on 3rd

Pitcher changes from the set position to the wind-up position without disengaging the pitcher's plate. This is a balk.

This is True.

6.02(b) Illegal pitches with bases unoccupied

1. Bases empty, 2 outs. Ball slips out of the pitcher's hand but does not cross the foul line.

   Is called a "no pitch".

---

2. Bases empty, 2 outs. Ball slips out of the pitcher's hand and crosses the foul line.

   Is called a ball.

---

3. Runner on 1st, 2 outs. Ball slips out of the pitcher's hand but does not cross the foul line.

   Is called a balk.

---

4. Runner on 1st, 2 outs. Ball slips out of the pitcher's hand and crosses the foul line.

   Is called a balk.

---

5. If a pitcher makes an illegal pitch with the bases unoccupied, it is a:

   Ball.

6.03 Batter Illegal Action

6.03(a) Batter out for Illegal Action

---

1. Batter hits a pitch fair while he has one foot on the ground entirely outside the batter's box:

   Batter is out.

---

2. Pitcher is in set position. Batter changes batter's boxes - going from hitting left-handed to right-handed before pitch is delivered.

   Batter is out.

   Batter may not change the side he is hitting from after the pitcher has become set.

---

3. Runner on 1st, no outs. Left-handed batter at the plate. Catcher attempts to pick runner off 1st base. Batter steps out of the batter's box and interferes with the catcher's attempt at the pick off.

   Batter is ruled out.

---

4. Runner on 1st, no outs. Left-handed batter at the plate. Catcher attempts to pick runner off 1st base. Batter steps out of the batter's box and interferes with the catcher's attempt at the pick off. Catcher recovers from the interference and throws out the runner at 1st. Batter is still out for his interference resulting in a double play.

   This is False.

   Batter is no longer out for interference when the runner is thrown out on the play.

---

5. Batter swings and makes contact with the pitch while half of his lead foot is outside the batter's box. He is out.

    This is False.

    To be called out, the batter must have one foot *entirely* outside the batter's box when he makes contact.

---

6. Batter hits a pitch foul while he has one foot on the ground entirely outside the batter's box. The batter is out.

    This is True.

    To be called out, the batter must have one foot entirely outside the batter's box when he makes contact, and the pitch can be hit either fair or *foul.*

6.03(b) Batting Out of Turn

---

1. Batter B bats out of order in Batter A's spot in the batting order. Batter B takes two strikes, and the defensive team then protests that Batter B is batting out of order.

    No out. Batter A comes to bat with 0 ball 2 strike count.

---

2. Bases empty, 1 out. Batter B bats out of order in Batter A's spot in the batting order. Batter B slaps a single to center field. The defensive team appeals to the umpire before the next pitch is made that Batter B was out of order.

    Batter A is ruled out. Batter following Batter A in batting order comes to bat.

---

3. Bases empty, 1 out. Batter B bats out of order in Batter A's spot in the batting order. Batter B slaps a single to center field. Defense does not realize Batter B is out of order and the pitcher makes a pitch to the next batter. Who is now the legal batter?

   Batter following Batter B in the lineup.

---

4. Runner on 1st, no outs. Batter B bats out of order in Batter A's spot in the batting order. Runner steals 2nd on the first pitch to Batter B (a strike taken by the batter). Batter B swings and misses on the next pitch. Defense then realizes Batter B is out of order and protests.

   No out. Batter A comes to bat with a 0 ball 2 strike count. Runner remains at 2nd base.

---

5. If the umpire notices a batter is batting out of order before either team brings attention to it, he should immediately call time and enforce the proper penalty for a player batting out of turn.

   This is False.

---

6. When a player bats out of turn (an improper batter), and a legal appeal is made by the defensive team:

   The proper batter is called out.

7.00 Ending the Game

7.01 Regulation Games

1. True or False. A game is called in the bottom of the 4th inning because of rain with the home team ahead. This is a regulation game.

   This is False

2. True or False. A game is called in the bottom of the 5th inning because of rain with the home team ahead. This is a regulation game.

   This is True

3. True or False. A game is called in the bottom of the 5th inning because of rain with the visiting team ahead. This is a regulation game.

   This is False

4. For an extra inning game, a runner will be placed on 2nd base to begin the inning for both teams starting in what inning (assuming 9 inning regulation game)?

   10th inning

5. What player is placed on 2nd base to begin the inning in an extra inning game?

   The player immediately preceding the leadoff hitter in the order (for example, if clean-up hitter is leading off the inning, 3rd place hitter in lineup becomes runner at 2nd).

6. True or False. If the umpire notices an improper runner is placed on 2nd base in an extra-inning game before either team brings attention to it, he should immediately bring attention to it and have the correct runner placed on base.

   This is True

7. A runner is placed on 2nd base to begin the top of the 10th inning. Batter hits first pitch for a single, and the runner from 2nd scores. Defensive correctly points out that incorrect runner was placed on 2nd base:

The run counts. Play continues with a runner on 1st base and no outs.

7.02 Suspended, Postponed, and Tie Games

1. True or False. A game is called in the bottom of the 3rd inning because of a *light failure* with the home team ahead. This becomes a suspended game.

   This is True

2. True or False. A game is called in the bottom of the 3rd inning because of a *local curfew* with the home team ahead. This becomes a suspended game.

   This is False

3. True or False. A game is called in the bottom of the 3rd inning because of *rain* with the home team ahead. This becomes a suspended game.

   This is True

4. True or False. A game is called in the top of the 6th inning because of rain with the score tied. This becomes a suspended game.

   This is True

8.00 The Umpire

8.01 Umpire Qualifications and Authority

1. True or False : Batter hits a screaming line drive down the 3rd base line. Base umpire rules it a fair ball. 3rd Baseman argues with the call, and is immediately ejected by the umpire. At the moment of the ejection, the ball is dead and all runners advance to the bases they would have reached, in the umpire's judgment, if the play was allowed to continue.

   This is False.

   If an umpire disqualifies a player while a play is in progress, the disqualification will not take effect until no further action is possible in that play.

8.02 Appeal of Umpire Decisions

1. True or False: Batter attempts to check his swing on a pitch outside the strike zone. Home plate umpire rules that he swung at the pitch. An appeal may be made that he did not swing.

   This is False.

   Appeals on a half swing may be made on the call of ball only. If the home plate umpire rules that the batter swung at the pitch, no appeal may be made.

2. True or False: Batter attempts to check his swing on a pitch outside the strike zone. Home plate umpire rules that he did not swing at the pitch. An appeal may be made to the base umpire that the batter swung.

   This is True.

   Appeals on a half swing may be made on the call of "no swing" and a ball is called by the home plate umpire

2023 Rule Changes not incorporated into a specific section

1. The pitch clock begins to count down for the pitcher when:

   Pitcher receives the ball.

2. With the bases empty, the pitch clock starts at **15** seconds.

3. With runners on base, the pitch clock starts at **20** seconds.

4. Batters must be in the batter's box and alert to the pitcher by the **8**-second mark on the pitch clock.

5. Pitchers are allowed **2** step-offs and/or pick-off attempts per plate appearance.

6. If pitcher exceeds his pick-off attempt limit for a particular runner, and does not pick off the runner on the play:

   A balk is called on the pitcher.

7. If pitcher exceeds his pick-off attempt limit for a particular runner, but picks off the runner on the play:

   No infraction is called.

8. Runner on 1st. Pitcher uses his maximum pick-off attempts for R1. R1 steals 2nd base. Pitcher is not allowed any pick-off attempts for the runner now on 2nd base.

   This statement is False.

Notes

Notes

Notes

Notes

Online Study Guideline

25 questions randomly drawn from all sections of the Official Rules.
    <u>At end of exam</u>:
    Shows pct correct for each section tested.
    Correct answers for each question viewed.
    Print certificate of completion when passing score (70%) is achieved.

Play an unlimited number of times.

Scan code below to PLAY ONLINE!!!!

secure.joyqr.com

Marathon Ump

Marathon Ump Mission Statement

We want to help youth baseball players follow their passion by providing the financial means to participate in their chosen sport(s), educating them on the rules and history of the sport, and providing access to the tools needed for their success.

Marathon Ump is proud to be a youth league umpire at the Texas Rangers Youth Academy's RBI (Reviving Baseball in Inner Cities) league.

The Texas Rangers Youth Academy provides free year-round baseball and softball instruction to athletes ages 7-18, summer ball through Major League Baseball's Nike RBI (Reviving Baseball in Inner Cities) League, dozens of on-field development opportunities and education programming for its athletes on their journey to becoming Major League citizens.

Opened in West Dallas in December 2017, the Texas Rangers Youth Academy at Mercy Street Sports Complex, presented by Toyota features five outdoor fields, batting cages, bullpens and the Globe Life Training Center, which houses an indoor field, classrooms, offices and a weight room.

Made in the USA
Las Vegas, NV
10 January 2024

84195886R00075